THE WORLD AS IT WAS

1865–1921

A Photographic Portrait from the Keystone-Mast Collection

Edited and with text by Margarett Loke
Foreword by Paul Theroux

SUMMIT BOOKS
NEW YORK

Acknowledgments

The majority of the prints for this book were made from the original glass negatives by Jerome D. Laval of Graphic Technology Company of Fresno, California, who, with Mead Kibbey, an alumnus of the University of California, was instrumental in arranging the donation of the Keystone collection to the California Museum of Photography at the University of California, Riverside. Chris Kenney, archivist of the Keystone-Mast Collection at the Museum, made many of the "last-minute" prints and assisted in researching the photographers and original publishers of the stereographs shown in this book.

Much of the background material on stereography was provided by Harvey B. Schneider of T. M. Visual Industries of New York City and William C. Darrah of Gettysburg, Pennsylvania, author of *The World of Stereographs,* who also kindly read the text on the collection in manuscript. Staff members of the Prints and Photographs Division of the Library of Congress, Tuskegee Institute and Vassar College generously offered their time to supply caption material, and the New York Public Library was indispensable in supplying historical material on the world between 1865 and 1921.

I am especially grateful for the many kindnesses and unfailing patience of Fred Ritchin, who offered invaluable assistance during the final selection of the stereographs; Ray Hooper, the book's designer; and Jonathan Segal, my editor.

Margarett Loke

May 1980

Foreword copyright © 1980 by Cape Cod Scriveners Company
Copyright © 1980 by Jerome D. Laval/Graphic Technology Company,
T.M. Visual Industries, Inc., and Margarett Loke
Published by SUMMIT BOOKS
A Simon & Schuster Division of Gulf & Western Corporation
Simon & Schuster Building, 1230 Avenue of the Americas
New York, New York 10020
SUMMIT BOOKS and colophon are trademarks of Simon & Schuster
Designed by Ray Hooper
Manufactured in the United States of America

1 2 3 4 5 6 7 8 9 10

Library of Congress Cataloging in Publication Data
Loke, Margarett.
   The world as it was.

   1. Civilization, Modern—19th century—Pictorial
works.   2. Civilization, Modern—20th century—
Pictorial works.   3. Photography, Artistic.
4. Photography, Stereoscopic.   I. Title.
CB417.L64   779'.990981   80-13031
ISBN 0-671-25376-X

Table of Contents

To my grandmother, in memory.

THE PAST RECAPTURED

By Paul Theroux

Memory often simplifies past events: the mind can be merciful. There is probably no greater burden than a capacity for total recall, but few of us are burdened in this way. We tend to be content with fragments of the past—the anecdote highly polished in the retelling, the once-painful vision given the soft focus (if not complete revision) of tranquil recollection—and we may smile when we are corrected and reminded that we have been betrayed by memory. It is certainly easier to reflect on experience as a monochrome or something prettified and made manageable by repetition. We might deliberately seek to uncover a complex image in our memory and find that time has turned it into a piffling snapshot. All we can do, if so much has been lost to us—so much discarded or altered —is turn our back on the past and flee it, setting our face at the abstraction of a dimly perceived future.

History can seem as simple as our personal past, and the memory's mechanism for simplifying can mislead us into believing history to be no more than anonymous leaders and featureless emblems, and historical change to have something to do with the algebra of dates or the inevitability of armies. We think of armies and we see ants. Even portraiture has been simplified into shapes, rather than the particularities in faces and clothes. Stalin is a fierce mustache and Lincoln a kindly beard, and the Tsaritsa's face is squeezed between diamonds; the peasant is barefoot, the African is naked. The warbonnet, the pigtail, the soldier wrapped in bandoliers—emblems. We may read biographies and histories and trek through museums, and still be convinced that "human history" is a bloodless phrase for an unreadable epoch.

We are left, then, with the anonymity of history. Compressed and robbed of subtlety, those who acted out the past are seen illustrating the most basic emotions—fear, triumph, hope, or greed—and nothing as fragile as fatigue, boredom, or compassion. Ultimately, because the past seems ungraspable, we may cease to care.

Photography did not kill painting ("From now on, painting is dead," the early photographers declared), but it caused its derangement into abstraction and—what seems much worse—made us unsure of realism, made us regard realism as inartistic. What we have seen lately is photography hurrying to compete with painting's abstraction, mimicking its postures and geometry. Many painters have succeeded in conveying a sense of power with color and line, even randomly—indeed, painting has never been able to be realistic

8

in a photographic way. But photographers huffing and puffing after painterly effects—I am thinking of the cubism of the New York photographer or the mess his European counterpart makes of photographic impressionism or the Japanese passion for dead branches —nearly always fail. Why should the exact science of optics be rivets, or a banana? The pity of it is that almost since its inception —the proof is in this book—photography has been able to give history a human face by supplying us with a crystal image.

The eye is selective, the camera lens is not; which is why photography, when it is masterly, is both an art and a science, the triumph of technology creating a luminous and symmetrical artifact. And it seems to me (though not to everyone) that what photography does best, when successful, is suggest imagination by dealing with the actual. Its subtlety is its exactitude, for in photography light is everything, and in light is its capacity for utter clarity. It is not necessary for the photographer to hedge or to fudge a plain image in an attempt at poetry. Because we know how untruthful a photograph can be, the photographer's integrity is crucial (and I may say that the famous picture of the flag-raising on Iwo Jima has always struck me as something of a phony, a sop to jingoism—it did not surprise me to learn that it was posed).

Of course, a photographer may take liberties. When Julia Margaret Cameron did her portrait of Herschel, she rumpled his crown of white hair beforehand to make him seem Jovian and astronomer-like. But her greatest photographs—like the best ones here—are those in which she practiced the keenest fidelity to her subject. It was not for nothing that Tennyson called the portrait she did of him "The Dirty Monk," but there does not exist a painting of the poet which has the smell and feel of that photograph—the grubby cape, the unkempt hair, the ragged beard. It does not diminish the poetry—on the contrary, we begin to see that Tennyson's sonorous verse was written by a hand with a human smell.

We have become accustomed to photographs of photographs, pictures of pictures, overlaid with dust and dead air. In the reprinting they have become coarsened and blurred, coarsening our own vision. Technically, it is often impossible to make photographs from original negatives, and the crystal image clouds in successive reproductions. We have even made the mistake of thinking of early photography as imperfect, slightly astigmatic, a primitive craft improved and modernized only recently. This is more than merely unfair—it belittles the skill of the 19th-century photographers and, in consequence, does violence to our idea of history. For who, looking through the pictures in this book, could have believed that stinks and perfumes could exist so sharply in portraiture, or that our own features could be mirrored like this?

It ought to have been apparent to us in reviewing the history of the past century that we were dealing with men and not gods, with dead soldiers and not casualty statistics. But to a large degree, we were cheated—given a foreground, or a full face, and denied the background, the periphery, the detail that tells more than the man at the focal point. "Focal point" itself is meaningless here, since the large plate camera and the long exposure allowed everything within its frame to be picked out. And it is details, particularities, that shock us, touch us, make us laugh, invite us to look closer—or, at any rate, make us understand what in the world we have lost.

I think we may have been in danger of forgetting how clear a photograph can be or how much paraphernalia it can contain. The picture of Booker T. Washington at Tuskegee is a fine family portrait—four faces with a lively intensity of gaze (this book is nothing if not a study of the human eye; when have we been so privileged to look the past in the eye?); but notice the wooden steps in the picture. We know at a glance they have been swept, that someone has climbed them and tracked dust on them; that they will be swept again. The dust is palpable. But this book has its share of statesmen and rulers with unreliable-looking expressions or wild, staring eyes, or the symptoms of illness. The panoply, the diamonds and costumes are never anything but grand—and yet see: Those are very human animals whom, until now, we have regarded as larger than life. Queen Victoria is pint-sized and pouting, and as she sits it seems that her feet do not reach to the ground.

In the schoolroom and factory and in the long dark line of workers waiting to be paid, the faces stare out helplessly, trapped by circumstances, and we feel judged, because we have never been gazed at in quite that way, so immediately, across time. Moments before many of these pictures were taken, the last words spoken were "Hold still!" We can see the effect of that command in the small boy's shoulders or the man's grip on the chair back. Everyone here is holding his breath, as if for a hundred-year leap to the present. And you want to weep after seeing some of these faces, or the conditions that are so obviously suffered. We have seen bare feet before—bare feet, as I said earlier, are the cliché emblem of the peasant. But look at the Russian peasants and much more than that is revealed, for we can almost be indifferent to bare feet, but cannot but be moved by those feet in the mud of that wet, mushy road. They are deeply physical, not at all anonymous, and this is the beginning of understanding, for they arouse not only simple concern, but compassion as well. We know, from this perspective, what happened to those people, why they revolted, how they fought or submitted, and how they died.

Photographic archives are full of pictures of beheadings. They were as much sought after and widely prized as movies or stills of modern executions. When a prisoner is electrocuted or shot today, the first frantic rapping on the door of the execution chamber is sure to be that of photographers or men with TV cameras. I have seen a number of photographs taken in the last century, usually in China, of beheadings. Invariably the sword is shown poised over the neck (sometimes the head has been struck off and it lies severed on the ground). There is one similar photograph in this book, of a garroting, taken in the Philippines. The seated man does not look unduly alarmed. He might be posing. Possibly it is a grim rehearsal; it is not really shocking.

But the beheading in China (page 45) is electrifying. We see more than the sword and the head. The man has been struck with the blade several times, and the executioner is tensed to take another blow. The condemned man, clearly bleeding—that is blood, not hair, coursing from his twisted face—is a goner. But look at the faces of the men who are holding his ropes and supporting his gibbet. This is hardly the routine event we have been taught took place in imperial China. These men are as close as we are (and we are seeing something the witnesses in the background are missing), and they wear expressions of terror and disbelief. The whole affair is as shocking to them as it is—one hopes—to us. This is the opposite of anonymity, and after the experience of this photograph one cannot think of such an execution as something taken for granted, a ritual which we can regard as conventional and commonplace. It is almost cathartic, for those wincing men are expressing our own shock.

Some of these photographs are fixed in time—the Panama Canal, Mark Twain at his billiard table, Mahatma Gandhi posing for an artist—but others are much older than their dates suggest. They give us access to the past. The Ainus, the Bedouin, the Irish peat carriers, the Wa-Kikuyu and American Indians—these might have been taken in the '80s or '90s of the last century, or even more recently, but we may be assured that for the preceding century, and perhaps for many centuries before, the people looked exactly like this. Our glimpse is not of people caught in a given year, but of an image carried away from a much remoter past, and a few decades before they were to change out of all recognition. And the photographic method, the revealing glass negative and the bulky, efficient camera let us see something of their surroundings, too—the hut, the foliage or, in the case of the pioneer woman in the poke bonnet, the whole of the Grand Canyon.

The art in some of these photographs is indisputable ("Vermeer," said one of the editors as we leafed through the paste-ups—it was the photograph of a Japanese woman at her spinning wheel), and this is appropriate, because by the time we turn the last page we believe we have recaptured the past, and in a distinctly Proustian way. In Proust's masterpiece, photographs are repeatedly used to verify an event or nail down a memory. Proust mentions stereoscopes as well, in speaking of how a passionate memory can be reexamined clearly much later: "as though one had placed it behind the glasses of a stereoscope."

That perception occurs in *The Guermantes Way*. A bit later in that same volume, and in one of his most powerful pieces of hyperbole, Proust speaks of kissing Albertine. This embrace takes several lushly written pages. The kiss is practically incomparable, but he risks one comparison. A kiss evokes so many things in such a new dimension, he says, that there is almost nothing to liken it to, "apart from the most recent applications of the art of photography." Photography like a kiss: it is a pretty conceit.

It is satisfying that the man who gave us the greatest novel about the process of memory lived when all of these pictures were taken, and thought well enough of stereographs to make a simile for his fiction. It would be presumptuous for me to promise that anyone going through this collection of photographs will have a Proustian experience, but it is certain that no one studying these memorable faces and landscapes will feel quite the same afterward in speaking of the world as it was.

About
The Collection

At the Crystal Palace Exhibition of 1851 in London, the first world's fair, the milling throngs saw a viewing device that was soon to become the world's first visual mass-entertainment medium. The stereoscope—so named by its inventor, English physicist Sir Charles Wheatstone—converted two almost identical photographs placed side by side into a scene of startling three-dimensional realism. Spurred by the personal interest of Queen Victoria in the intriguing instrument and its views, opticians raced to manufacture stereoscopes, and stereo photographers roamed the world for better and more exotic pictures.

By 1858, the London Stereoscopic Company had 100,000 titles, and shops throughout Europe were selling stereoscopic views, the subjects ranging from monuments, vistas and portraits to visual slapstick, wars and faraway places. Then, in 1859, when the American physician, poet and essayist Oliver Wendell Holmes and his friend and fellow Bostonian Joseph L. Bates constructed the hand-held stereoscope, America became the center of stereoscopic activity. (The earlier stereoscopes were bulky, boxlike instruments that were far less convenient to handle and far more expensive.)

At the turn of the century, four of the largest producers of stereo views—called "stereographs" by Holmes—were B. W. Kilburn of Littleton, New Hampshire; Underwood and Underwood of New York; H. C. White Company of North Bennington, Vermont; and Keystone View Company of Meadville, Pennsylvania. Underwood, the leading publisher, was producing 25,000 stereo images a day, 300,000 stereoscopes a year.

Keystone, in 1892 the last of the four to enter the race, monopolized the field less than a decade later. By 1923 it had acquired the entire stock of its three principal competitors, and throughout the 1920s and 1930s it was the only major publisher of stereographs in the world, holding more than two million negatives in 1936. But during these decades, the company was competing not only against radio but against the latest magical entertainment medium —the motion picture. In 1913, three partners—Cecil B. DeMille, Jesse L. Lasky and Samuel Goldfish (who was soon to change his name to Goldwyn)—had moved from the East Coast to Hollywood. D. W. Griffith released *The Birth of a Nation* in 1915, and four years later, Griffith, Mary Pickford, Douglas Fairbanks and Charlie Chaplin formed United Artists. *The Jazz Singer,* the first feature film with synchronized sound, was shown in 1927. It was stunningly successful.

By the 1930s, stereo views, like silent movies, were relics of the

An H. C. White stereographer
perched with his camera on a steel
column of a new skyscraper,
New York City.

past. Keystone finally ceased regular production in 1939, the year that television was introduced at the New York World's Fair. About 350,000 glass negatives and prints were placed in three concrete vaults in Meadville. And there they lay, virtually forgotten by the photographic world, until March 1977, when the collection was donated to the California Museum of Photography at the University of California, Riverside, by the family of the late Gifford Mast of Davenport, Iowa, whose firm had acquired the Keystone View Company in 1963.

With the addition of the Keystone-Mast Collection, the California Museum of Photography suddenly became the third largest photographic museum in the United States, after the Smithsonian Institution and the International Museum of Photography at George Eastman House. Established in 1973, the university museum has among its holdings the Bingham Collection of early and modern photographic equipment, as well as a growing collection of vintage photographs and negatives, including the work of Henry Fox Talbot—the Englishman who, in 1839, was one of the inventors of photography—and such noted 20th century photographers as Gertrude Käsebier, Edward Weston and Ansel Adams.

•

The Keystone-Mast Collection is the largest of its kind to survive the era when the stereoscope was part of almost every home in the world touched by Western civilization.

In the few decades before the turn of the century, the far-flung corners of the world were for the first time more readily accessible. Extended railway connections, faster ships and the completion of the Suez Canal in 1869 helped. As did the West's "opening up" of China and Japan and its colonization of much of the rest of the world. The relentless pursuit of markets and colonies by the industrialized countries fanned a curiosity about other lands among the growing middle class, but with foreign travel still limited to a privileged few, the vast numbers bound to the land, factory or office could, through the stereograph, see people, places and things outside the pale of their everyday existence. In 1859, Oliver Wendell Holmes glowingly described the stereograph as "the card of introduction to make all mankind acquaintances."

An Underwood stereographer preparing to take a view of the crater of Asosan, central Kyushu, Japan, 1904.

Stereographers amassed an unprecedented visual record of 19th and early 20th century life, a record that is closely tied to the history of photography. When Wheatstone demonstrated his stereoscope in 1838—a year before the photographic processes developed by Louis Jacques Mandé Daguerre and Henry Fox Talbot were announced—he had used hand-drawn pictures for viewing. With the commercial development of photography, and the use of photographic prints for stereoscopic viewing, the stereoscopic industry was born. A dual-lens camera—manufactured commercially in 1854 and employing a single negative, usually 4 by 7 inches in size—simulated the perspectives seen by the left and right eyes; when a stereo card made from the two images was inserted in a stereoscope, the prismatic lenses of the viewer fused the two images into a single three-dimensional picture.

The stereo photographers' line of work was a particularly arduous one. To reach destinations that were not served directly by railroads or ships, they frequently had to travel over rough terrain. Once there, they could take one to two hours making one view, spending most of the time packing and unpacking photographic equipment. There were photographic tents, large dual-lens cameras (and often larger single-lens cameras as well, accommodating plates that were 10 by 12 inches or even 20 by 24 inches in size), tripods, generous supplies of glass plates packed in wooden boxes, chemicals, airtight glass jars for developing and fixing, and the portable darkroom that went with the collodion, or "wet plate," process, which became popular with photographers from the 1860s on.

The earlier photographic processes, the daguerreotype and the calotype, had their limitations. Both required long exposures. With the daguerreotype, the image made on a sensitized silver-plated sheet of copper could not be reproduced. While the calotype permitted positives to be printed from a single negative, its inventor, Henry Fox Talbot, restricted its use through patents. The collodion process, developed by F. Scott Archer in 1848, not only produced a negative, but used materials that were cheaper and easier to obtain than those required for a daguerreotype. What was more, wet collodion needed a fraction of the exposure time required by either the daguerreotype or the calotype, and there were no patent restrictions. Its drawback was that the glass negative had to be developed while the collodion emulsion was wet.

The photographers of the day had to have a high degree of manual dexterity. Before making an exposure, a photographer had to clean a sheet of glass, pour the liquid collodion over it, immerse the coated plate in silver nitrate to make it light-sensitive, position it in a plate-holder and insert the plate-holder in the camera. Immediately after the exposure was made, he had to develop the glass negative quickly.

Although George Eastman popularized the gelatin dry-plate process—an invention of English physician Richard Leach Maddox in 1871—by improving the exposure time and marketing his own mechanically coated plates, many photographers in the 1880s preferred to haul darkroom equipment with them, since the dry plate was still slower than wet collodion. It wasn't until the last few years of the 19th century that photographers could dispense with the portable darkroom.

•

Stereography, like its 20th century successor television, was entertaining and soporific, classy and vulgar, educational and sophomoric. Stereographs advertised products, entered the classroom as visual aids, were given away as premiums or were bought as reminders, like postcards, of a time and place. They showed the museum collections of Europe and every notable building and monument in the world in existence between 1850 and 1930. Stereographers followed Roald Amundsen to the South Pole and Gold Rush prospectors to Alaska. They staged biblical tableaux and scenes from Shakespeare and Dickens. Niagara Falls was more frequently stereographed than any other subject in the world; Britain was the most completely stereographed country. Of all the titles it pub-

Underwood photographer James Ricalton shown with two giants of Kashmir (the taller of the two is 7 feet 9 inches in height) at the Great Durbar of 1903, Delhi, India.

lished, Keystone sold the largest number of views of the wreckage of the U.S.S. *Maine.*

In the first few decades of stereography, three of its most noted practitioners were Francis Frith, William Henry Jackson and Eadweard Muybridge. Frith's views of Egypt, published by Negretti & Zambra of London in the late 1850s, were the most critically acclaimed series in the history of stereography. Jackson's stereo views of Yellowstone in the 1870s were instrumental in passage of the bill that created Yellowstone National Park. And Muybridge —whose photographic studies of animal locomotion led to the development of motion pictures—was in the 1860s and early '70s a stereographer who produced excellent views of Yosemite, San Francisco and the Modoc Indians.

(All three men also did exceptional work in single-image photography, but because of the wide distribution of stereo views and their enormous popularity, Frith and Jackson were famous before the turn of the century for their work in stereography. During the past few decades, when stereography has been little more than a footnote in the history of photography, these men have become known almost exclusively as single-image photographers.)

American stereographers differed from their English counterparts in one striking respect: the English placed more emphasis on panoramic scenery, architectural studies and studio poses, seldom recording disasters or offering views of community life. It wasn't until Underwood sent a photographer to Ireland shortly before the turn of the century that there appeared stereographs of Irish cottagers, peat cutters, workers and children.

The American public appeared to have a penchant for views of disasters, natural or man-made, and stereographers fed that morbid curiosity. They covered the Chicago fire of 1871, the most destructive in American history; the disastrous fire in Boston the next year; the Johnstown flood of 1889. After 1900, it was possible to get to scenes of destruction quickly, and American stereographers flocked to sites that had just seen volcanic eruptions or earthquakes.

Among the most important documentary photographs to emerge from the era of the stereoscope are the war views. Largely through the efforts of one man, Mathew B. Brady, the first major conflict to be systematically photographed—albeit from the Union side only —was the American Civil War. (Stereographs of the Confederate armies are very rare.) Hoping to make a profit from the sale of stereo views of the war, Brady made the majority of his war views on stereographic negatives and at times sent as many as twenty photographers into the field. But his practice of issuing all photographs under his own name angered some who worked for him; when Alexander Gardner separated from Brady in 1863 and established his own studio, he carefully credited each negative to the individual photographer. At the end of the war, Brady was badly in debt; sales of his views were sluggish, since the public simply wanted to forget the conflict.

When the Great War broke out, no war correspondent or civilian photographer was allowed near the Western Front: the penalty for taking pictures there was death. In 1914 Underwood photographers were active in Belgium and Flanders, but Keystone was unable to obtain permission from the War Department to send a photographer to France until the Armistice had been signed. After 1915, when all photographs were pooled, anonymity became the rule.

Press censorship, which lasted for the duration of the Great War, was a common feature in Europe throughout the 19th and early 20th centuries. During this period of political turmoil, it was necessary in many European countries to obtain from the police a permit to own or use a camera.

In the United States, where there was no muzzling of the press, many stereographers practiced a form of self-censorship. There were the occasional views of the appalling work conditions in many factories, but photography as an instrument for social reform was left to such contemporary photojournalists as Jacob Riis and Lewis W. Hine.

To a large extent, stereographers reflected in their work the conservative mind-set and tastes of the vast middle class that purchased their views. This is nowhere more evident than in the photographs of Victorian still-life arrangements, in the sentimental studio compositions depicting courtship, marriage or children (at play, saying their bedtime prayers, or asleep), and in the comic sets with their inevitable termagant wives and philandering husbands.

Social stereotyping was common. When blacks were not cast in comic sets—their very manner of speech was somehow hilarious to white viewers—they were shown as laborers. A stereograph of black lumbermen in Virginia had this caption: "Felling timbers in dismal swamp. The heat is so intense and yellow flies and mosquitoes so obnoxious that only Negroes can perform the work." On the back of a 1905 stereo card depicting Korean charcoal carriers is this descriptive, or "educational," material: "[Koreans] are quite a distinct race from their neighbors, the Chinese and Japanese. They are not all alike, as the Chinese, but are easily distinguished as individuals. They are generally cheerful in expression, and a little puzzled. They have quick intelligence but no great force of will."

And in the same way that, at a later time, movies would romanticize the American cowboy, stereographers sold the myth of the strong, silent hero of the Golden West. The text, for instance, found on the back of a stereo view of a 1902 roundup on a ranch in Kansas read in part: ". . . Prosperous farmers add hourly to their own and the nation's wealth, and sturdy ranchmen are among the most virile men in the world. From such rugged horsemen as the picture shows Roosevelt formed the Rough Riders who fought in Cuba and who, to speak in a figure, escorted their Colonel to the White House steps."

•

The vast majority of stereographers worked anonymously, a good number of them producing views of uncommon sensitivity and artistry. The men who began the publishing companies in the Keystone-Mast Collection either were or became photographers (like Brady, they generally did not give by-lines to their field

A daguerreotypist accompanied Commodore Matthew Perry on his second trip to Japan, in 1854, to "open" the country to the West. From the next decade on, professional photographic activity flourished in the principal cities of Japan, and European stereographers were soon competing against their Japanese counterparts, who included Renjo Shimooka, the first Japanese commercial photographer to open a studio (around 1859, in Yokohama), and Hikoma Uyeno, who became the most prestigious photographer in Nagasaki in the decades before 1900. Shown below is a Keystone stereoscopic view of a group of Japanese women taking turns viewing stereo cards through a stereoscope.

photographers). Benjamin West Kilburn, whose brother, Edward, started the Kilburn Company in 1865, took thousands of views throughout America, Europe and the Near East. After nine years spent merchandising stereo views with his brother, Elmer, Bert Underwood in 1891 took a few lessons in photography and quickly became a master of the craft. He photographed Upper Egypt in 1896; at the coronation of Nicholas II, he was granted permission to photograph the royal family. The founder of the Keystone View Company, B. Lloyd Singley, was an amateur photographer.

H. C. White, the world's principal manufacturer of hand-held stereoscopes in 1874, began publishing stereographs in 1899, producing prints of high quality. Carlton H. Graves, a photographer since the 1870s, was unable to compete with the aggressive marketing techniques of Kilburn and Underwood, and in the 1890s his work, as well as that of a few other photographers, was handled by a cooperative photoprinting facility in Bettsville, Ohio. The cooperative failed, and between 1897 and 1910, Graves published under a number of imprints.

One of the few staff stereographers to be identified by name was James Ricalton. A prolific Underwood photographer, Ricalton produced consistently excellent views. At the turn of the century, he covered the Spanish-American War in the Philippines and traveled to Hong Kong, then to China, where the views he took of the Boxer Rebellion were among the most graphic war views published up to that time. Ricalton was in Delhi for the Great Durbar (1903), and the Underwood India set of 100 of his negatives reveals an unerring sense of scenic interest and human drama.

The "boxed set" introduced by Underwood was widely imitated by its competitors. The set was a selection of a series of cards, usually 100, which included scenes of town and country, industry, agriculture, topography and people—scenes that would simulate a tour to a particular country. Captions for the Underwood sets were printed in six languages: English, French, German, Spanish, Russian and Swedish. A boxed set of 100 cards on China, which came with eight maps and a book by Ricalton titled *China Through the Stereoscope,* sold for $17.50. Underwood's aluminum-mahogany stereoscope was sold for about $1. Modest 15-card travel sets that came with a descriptive book and three maps sold for $2.50. Views were marketed with considerable zeal by traveling salesmen or distributed through large retail mail-order companies.

•

Stereographs have been described as "mediating romantic ideals and harsh realities." Like television today, stereography owed much of its immense commercial success to a society predisposed to what it offered.

—M.L.

PART I
THE AGE OF INCREDULITY
1865–1900

It was the best of times, it was the worst of times, it was the age of wisdom, it was the age of foolishness, it was the epoch of belief, it was the epoch of incredulity, it was the season of Light, it was the season of Darkness, it was the spring of hope, it was the winter of despair, we had everything before us, we had nothing before us . . .
A Tale of Two Cities, by Charles Dickens (1859)

While the rest of the world lived much as it had for centuries, even millennia, a handful of nations in Europe as well as a fledgling republic in North America took themselves out of the 19th century and moved into the 20th.

With considerable aplomb. For the revolutionaries of the age— scientists, philosophers, inventors and other visionaries—were an astonishing lot, many of whom would, in the first few decades of the next century, radically alter the lives of peoples throughout the world.

Interjected as they were into the orderly world of the Victorians —where everything, it seemed, from atoms to people, knew its place in the natural scheme of things—the new ideas and discoveries were often rudely unsettling.

If Charles Darwin's theory of evolution removed human beings from the exalted position of being "a little lower than the angels," Karl Marx's *Das Kapital* damned the capitalist system for reducing the working man or woman "to the level of an appendage of a machine."

And if Sigmund Freud shocked the Victorians by refusing to say exactly what was healthy and what was neurotic behavior, or to draw clear lines between normal and perverted sexuality, Friedrich Nietzsche went a step further, deeming the bourgeois society, and all its conventions, contemptible, and its idea of a benevolent God absurd. "I think of myself as the scrawl," he wrote, "which an unknown power scribbles across a sheet of paper, to try out a new pen."

Of course, the discoveries of the day were not always so traumatic in effect. Physicist Heinrich Hertz discovered electric (radio) waves in 1887, and less than a decade later, another physicist, Guglielmo Marconi, invented wireless telegraphy.

Ushering in the new world of atomic physics were four discoveries made between 1895 and 1898: X-rays by Wilhelm Conrad Roentgen, the radioactive property of uranium by Henri Becquerel, radium by Marie and Pierre Curie, and electrons by Joseph John Thomson.

In the field of chemistry, Sir William Ramsay became the first scientist to discover a whole group of new gaseous elements: argon, helium, neon, krypton and xenon. Adolf von Baeyer succeeded in 1880 in producing the first chemical synthesis of indigo—long one of the wildest dreams of a chemist. While Henri Moissan, winner of the Nobel Prize for chemistry in 1906, failed in his experiments to produce artificial diamonds, a Japanese marine farmer by the name of Kokichi Mikimoto not only was successful in producing his first semispherical artificial pearl in 1893, but he went on to perfect the spherical pearl. (Since the 13th century, the Chinese had been producing "blister pearls" which required the addition of half-spheres of mother-of-pearl to give them the rounded pearl form.)

In medicine, Louis Pasteur's research in disease-causing microbes spearheaded the conquest of such age-old decimators of the human race as the plague, cholera, tuberculosis, diphtheria and scarlet fever. Working along the lines of Pasteur's germ theory of infection, Joseph Lister made the first use of an antiseptic in 1865 and inaugurated the modern era of surgery.

Alexander Graham Bell patented his "talking box" in 1876. Three years later, Thomas A. Edison perfected a long-lasting incan-

descent light bulb—something that had eluded other inventive minds for 200 years—and then devised a system for distributing electricity to individual homes, much as gas was distributed. Earlier, in 1877, Edison had invented a machine to record and reproduce sound, which he called the phonograph.

For the textile industry, the greatest single innovation was the automatic loom, developed in the early 1890s. For farmers, industrialization produced, in the 1880s, the revolutionary reaper-thresher, or combine, which reaped, threshed, cleaned and bagged the grain in a single continuous operation, making it possible for four men to do the work of three hundred.

A flurry of office equipment sprang into being: the ticker tape (1867), typewriter (1868), mimeograph machine and cash register (1876), adding machine (1888). By the 1890s, there were, for the home, such labor-saving electrical devices as the fan, iron, coffeepot, cigar lighter and stew pan.

The "Rover," the predecessor of the modern safety bicycle, was produced by James K. Starley in England in 1885. About that time, two men, Gottlieb Daimler, a German industrial engineer, and Karl Benz, a German inventor, working independently, developed similar internal-combustion engines, mounted them on vehicles and successfully operated them. But it was Emile Levassor, of the French firm of Panhard and Levassor, a French carriage builder and licensee of the Daimler motor vehicle, who built, in the 1890s, what became the prototype for the entire industry: he positioned the engine in front of the chassis (since the horse had been in front) and developed the clutch, gearbox and transmission.

The electric car was popular in the 1890s, but in 1896, a former machinist's apprentice turned automobile designer (who supported himself and his wife by working at the Edison Illuminating Company in Detroit) built a successful gasoline-powered vehicle. His name was Henry Ford.

In 1896 Samuel Pierpont Langley, American astronomer and physicist, made a steam-driven, pilotless airplane, which he called an aerodrome and which flew a distance of 4,200 feet over the Potomac River.

It is perhaps symptomatic of the spirit of the time that in the 1860s Jules Verne, dreaming of submarines, aircraft and television, should write *Voyage au centre de la terre* and *Vingt mille lieues sous les mers*, and that, as the 19th century drew to a close, H. G. Wells, with visions of another future age, should write *The Time Machine, The War of the Worlds* and *The First Men in the Moon*.

•

Telegraph cables and railroad tracks, crisscrossing nations and continents, made the world a much smaller place than it was at the beginning of the 19th century. And, paradoxically, European and American companies buying and selling the products of this diminished world became Brobdingnagian. Unencumbered by such metaphysical concerns as moral obligations, the corporations of the modern industrialized state had only one objective—to make money, lots of it, quickly, efficiently. Starting in the 1880s, corporations (which were themselves combinations of big businesses) combined to form trusts, which had two objectives: to create monopolies and to make even more money.

John D. Rockefeller's Standard Oil Company became the first trust in 1882. Mergers were necessary, said the former produce bookkeeper, "to save ourselves from wasteful competition." In 1886 Alfred Nobel established the first international trust—the Dynamite Trust Limited. Soon, corporations and trusts in Europe and America were engaged in a furious—and often vicious—race to monopolize every conceivable commodity, from tobacco to zinc, from oil to buttons.

To match the power of private interests, governments in turn took on all the trappings of a corporation as they embarked for the first time on a comprehensive regulation of society, especially in the areas of public health, elementary education, working conditions and control of public utilities. As time went on, governments fabricated such elaborate layers of bureaucracy that they outdid the corporations in impersonality.

Trade unions—previously craft organizations whose members were skilled workers in special trades—were now organized on a national scale and by industries. They too suffered from giantism. Adopting the principle of the corporate model—the divorce of power from social responsibility—organized labor looked to its own interests with little concern for the wider consequences of its actions.

The industries of the corporate society formed in the four decades before 1900 created an increasing atomization of labor, just as they produced the most degraded environment the world had yet seen. The industrial blight of England in the early 19th century was exported to America. Land was gouged and stripped to make room for railways; mountains were catacombed with mine shafts or leveled so that their ore could be extracted; rivers, streams and lakes became the dumping grounds for industrial wastes, and foul clouds of smoke hovered over the cities.

The corporate society saw for the first time a phenomenon that was unknown in preindustrial days: recurring cycles of national depressions and recessions, price declines and fluctuations. Ironically, while the corporate society destroyed the tight-knit communities of old and made strangers of neighbors, it created an interlocking economic system that mercilessly bound people, and countries, together. The failure of any major corporation not only threw thousands out of work, it adversely affected other business sectors: suppliers, jobbers, retailers, transportation companies.

Immune to the vicissitudes of the marketplace during these decades were the members of the new aristocracy—the industrial tycoons. The United States, given its special circumstances—it was a young, developing land and had seemingly inexhaustible resources—produced a disproportionate number of fabulously wealthy men as it made its meteoric transformation from a rural republic to the greatest industrial nation of the world: Andrew Carnegie, John D. Rockefeller, J. P. Morgan, Henry Clay Frick, Jay Gould, Cornelius Vanderbilt, Collis P. Huntington, Leland Stanford, Mark Hopkins, William C. Whitney, James B. Duke, Meyer Guggenheim.

Accumulating more wealth more quickly than any potentate of an earlier time, the nouveaux riches ushered in an era of legendary extravagance (economist and social scientist Thorstein Veblen dubbed the practice "conspicuous consumption" in 1899). "Marble House" in Newport, a gift from William K. Vanderbilt to his wife, Alva, featured rare marble from Africa and a ballroom paneled in gold. Besides racehorses and yachts, August Belmont, banker and owner of the Belmont racing stables, owned a railroad car staffed with a French chef. "A private railroad car," said his second wife, Eleanor, "is not an acquired taste. One takes to it immediately."

Between the new aristocracy (who were permitted their baroque flights of fancy since great wealth supposedly conferred on them special privileges that were denied ordinary people) and the poor (who were, according to popular thought, shiftless, imbecilic creatures) was a burgeoning "middle class" known for being "hardworking," "thrifty" and "respectable." As industries and governments required more and more managers, technicians, clerical workers, social workers, public-health officials, teachers, doctors, lawyers, urban planners, ad infinitum, the bourgeoisie became the dominant class. Queen Victoria herself seemed the epitome of the middle class, possessing as she did such sterling bourgeois qualities as uncomplicated devoutness, unyielding respectability, common sense and boundless diligence.

The middle class—within whose ranks could be found what social Darwinist William Graham Sumner called "the forgotten man" and what was later to be called "the silent majority"—was viewed, however, by its detractors as a class that was not only devoid of creativity and taste but was repressive, hypocritical and narrow-minded to boot. Theirs was the kind of sensibility which recoiled at the "low doings" on stage when Bizet's *Carmen* premiered at the Opéra Comique in Paris in 1875, and which condemned the copper statue of Diana the Huntress—the crowning glory of the second Madison Square Garden—as an "undraped hussy" and indicative of "the depraved artistic taste of New York." (The statue, by Augustus Saint-Gaudens, now stands atop the grand staircase in the Philadelphia Museum of Art.)

While the middle class held fast to those virtues that were considered conducive to wholesome family life, the working masses—most of whom were paid a pittance for long, repetitious, deadening work—were already seeing their families disintegrate as the women and children were forced to work as well. While industrialization symbolized all that was progressive and bountiful to the middle and upper classes, for many of the lowliest workers it was hell on earth. From crowded, ill-ventilated workplaces they went to crowded, ill-ventilated homes—to those urban tenements whose nearest counterparts were the slave ships of old, where human cargoes were packed into every available inch of space, where sanitation facilities were nonexistent, where the very air was foul. H. L. Mencken remembered a Baltimore which smelled "like a billion polecats," and which was devastated by "a great epidemic of typhoid fever every summer, and a wave of malaria every autumn, and more than a scattering of smallpox . . . every winter."

The poor were offered scant relief when unemployment, illness, injury or death left their families with nothing but the horrors of the poorhouse or slow starvation. Effectively delaying improvement in welfare for the poor was a belief—rooted in Puritanism—that poverty was due to individual fault. Using Darwin's theory of the survival of the fittest, English philosopher Herbert Spencer promulgated the notion that "the artificial preservation of those least able to take care of themselves" was contrary to the principle of natural selection. To which American sociologist Lester Ward countered in 1893 that "if nature progresses through the destruction of the weak, man progresses through the protection of the weak."

Gradually, Ward's view on poor relief replaced that of the social Darwinists. Recurrent depressions convinced many that poverty might be the result of adverse economic and social systems and not the result of laziness or an inferior mind. Newspapers and books reported the abysmal conditions in factories and tenements to increasing numbers of readers. There was fear, too, that without relief the poor might join the socialists, Communists and anarchists in fomenting revolutions. A German system of social insurance, sponsored by Chancellor Otto von Bismarck in 1881 and codified in 1911 in the Workmen's Insurance Code, began in part as an attempt to "save" the German working classes from "the siren song of socialism."

The British Parliament passed the Workmen's Compensation

Act in 1897, but it wasn't until 1948 that Britain eradicated the last traces of its Elizabethan poor laws by the enactment of the National Assistance Act. In America, it took the Great Depression of the 1930s to jolt the Federal Government into writing into law public assistance, unemployment compensation, social security benefits and other welfare legislation for the country.

•

These were desperate times for peoples and nations without the means of swift conquest or defense. Viewed either as *terra nullius* (to be claimed by the first "civilized" person who came along) or "backward" (that is, vulnerable to modern Western weaponry), these lands—in the Near East, southern Asia, Africa, the Pacific and the Far East—in four short decades became the domain of half a dozen empires, and their peoples became known, whenever they were uncooperative, as "heathen savages."

Equipped with the best armaments a modern industrial age could give them—iron-and-steel ships, heavier naval guns, machine

guns, more accurate rifles—the latter-day Conquistadors nonetheless employed curiously medieval tactics in "opening up" China and Japan, two ancient and highly civilized imperial nations that had, until the mid-19th century, repeatedly and effectively shunned the overtures of the barbarians of the West for extended trade.

All that a Western power had to do was sail up the harbor of a Chinese or Japanese city, warships belching black smoke, and treaties would be hastily signed. These were not treaties signed between equals; as befitted the status of an "advanced" nation dealing with "inferior" races, each Western power signing treaties with China or Japan made provisions for low tariffs on imports (which could not be changed except with the consent of the foreign power) and extraterritoriality (which meant that Westerners residing in China or Japan were not subject to the law of the land but remained under the jurisdiction of their respective homelands). Any infraction against persons or property of a Western power brought swift and savage revenge: the retaliatory bombardment or sacking of cities; more ports opened to Western trading; more concessions; heavy indemnities.

China and Japan reacted to such humiliations in diametrically opposite ways. Accustomed to viewing other states not as equals but as tributaries, China was slow to see any merit in the industrialized ways of the barbarians or to recognize that the only way to ward them off was to beat them at their own game. But even when reforms were finally seen as necessary, the Chinese were caught between the machinations of the Borgia-like Empress Dowager Tzu Hsi and the inept and corrupt officials whose overriding sense of self-preservation precluded any meaningful change.

The Japanese, threatened by modern military might, overthrew the feeble Tokugawa shogunate and in 1868 restored the Emperor Meiji to his full authority. Thereupon, they embarked on an ambitious program of modernization. By 1894, equipped with modern weapons, Japan was able to wage a successful war against China, which was forced to cede to its former vassal the island of Formosa and to pay an indemnity of 200 million taels in silver.

Japan, which so quickly demonstrated that it could make itself over in the image of the modern European nations, and play the imperialist game as well as the best of them, was a lesson to the Western powers: the same reforms could not be allowed to take place in China, which, following its humiliating defeat by Japan, was frantically planning modernization programs of its own. In 1898 Germany, Russia, France, Britain and Italy scrambled for further concessions, gaining "spheres of influence" in thirteen of China's eighteen richest provinces.

Alarmed that China might soon be divided into exclusive spheres (or worse, that areas of it might actually be annexed by Japan or Russia, the nearest big-power neighbors), the United States announced its policy of the "open door." In essence, it meant that for China to remain open to the trading of all Western nations, it would stay "territorially intact."

Extraterritoriality, which had become a fact of life for China since the 1840s, had long been established in the Ottoman Empire. Since the loss of Hungary in 1699, the empire had been slowly disintegrating. At the Congress of Berlin—convened by Bismarck after the Russo-Turkish war of 1877–78—the European powers decided that Serbia, Rumania and Montenegro would be granted their independence; Bosnia would be "occupied and administered" by Austria-Hungary; Cyprus would be ceded to Britain, and the French would expand their influence from Algeria into Tunisia. As in China, the Ottoman Empire's attempts at reforms in the 1860s and 1870s were ineffectual because of powerful internal—and external—resistance to radical change.

As casually and arrogantly as they had dismembered the Ottoman Empire, the European powers carved up the Dark Continent. Beginning in the 1880s with Henry M. Stanley, who had been sent by the *New York Herald* to find David Livingstone in 1871 and who had subsequently managed to engage the interest of Leopold II, King of the Belgians, in developing the Congo, explorers negotiated treaties with African chiefs as they traveled inland from the coasts—the treaties in effect allowing them to claim territorial sovereignty for European powers. When territorial claims began to overlap, Bismarck (who considered the acquisition of African colonies an absurdity) called another conference. Blithely ignoring the territorial sovereignty of the native inhabitants, the 1885 Congress of Berlin made Leopold II sole ruler of the Congo Free State (an area almost the size of the United States east of the Mississippi), declared the Congo River an international body of water, and stipulated that while any European power with holdings on the coast had prior rights to the backcountry, all holdings had to be occupied by administrators or troops and its borders clearly indicated to other European powers.

This last item set off another mad scramble. By 1900 the continent was largely in the hands of the leading empire builders.

◆

The Industrial Society

At no other period in history had the world come into possession
so quickly of so huge an increase in its natural wealth. And America—more than
any European country, with the possible exception of Russia—had an awesome
abundance of such raw materials as iron ore, copper, coal and oil. By
1890, American production of iron and steel surpassed that of Britain, and
Andrew Carnegie's Homestead Steel plant in Pennsylvania was the
largest in the nation. Its workers—mostly Southern and Eastern European immigrants—
worked twelve hours a day, seven days a week, in an inferno of heat and noise.

View of Homestead Steel works, Pennsylvania. By H. C. White.

Homestead workers waiting to be paid.
By H. C. White.

Boys picking slate in a breaker in an
anthracite coal mine in Pittsburgh, Pennsylvania.
By Underwood and Underwood.

From 1881 to 1905, there were no fewer
than 37,000 strikes in the United
States. One of the most spectacular
was the Homestead strike of 1892,
when Pinkerton guards hired by Henry
Clay Frick, a Carnegie associate,
fought a pitched battle with the strikers.
Not only had Carnegie proposed to make
the plant nonunion that year, but Frick
had suggested a wage cut as well. After
the strikers drove off the Pinkertons,
8,000 National Guardsmen were sent in
by the Governor to restore order.

*Overleaf: Homestead workers' homes overlooking
the steel plant. By H. C. White.*

Andrew Carnegie with his pet dog. By Underwood and Underwood.

Railroads were vital to the surging industrial revolution taking place in Europe, America and Japan. Europe's main railway systems were completed by the early 1870s, and during the next three decades the network was extended to Constantinople, Salonica and Vladivostock. In the United States, railways were an efficient means of transport and the civilizers of the Western frontier. Between 1865 and 1890, about 70,000 miles of railroad were added; by 1900, there was a total of about 200,000 miles of railway—making up the greatest railroad system of any country in the world.

Train passing over a trestle, 1891. By B. W. Kilburn.

Dining car of the Pennsylvania Limited, c. 1889.

Before Thomas Edison's death in 1931, at the age of 84, the U.S. Patent Office had granted him 1,098 patents, which included those for a ticker system (for which he was paid $40,000 when he was still 21), a carbon transmitter (which helped make the Bell telephone a practicable device, and for whose use Western Union paid Edison $100,000), the phonograph, and the incandescent light bulb (which made him a national celebrity at the age of 32). Guglielmo Marconi's invention of wireless telegraphy in 1895, when he was 21, led to the creation of commercial radio in Britain and America in the early 1920s. George Washington Carver, who was born of slave parents during the Civil War, freed Southern farmers from a ruinous one-crop (cotton) economy by persuading them to diversify their crops and plant soil-enriching peanuts and sweet potatoes. He solved the problem of finding uses for these crops by demonstrating that peanuts yielded 300 products; sweet potatoes, some 118 products.

Guglielmo Marconi, the inventor of wireless telegraphy.

George Washington Carver in his research laboratory at Tuskegee Institute, Alabama. By Phil Brigandi of Keystone View Company.

Thomas Alva Edison with his wife, Mina, daughter, Madeline, and sons Theodore and Charles (standing) at their home in Llewellyn Park, New Jersey. By Underwood and Underwood.

Fountains in front of the Palace of Electricity, Paris Exposition, 1900. By H. C. White.

Once more, the *exposition internationale* lay at the feet of that giant monument of modernism, the Eiffel Tower, which had been raised for the exposition of 1889 at a cost of 15 million francs—even though 300 of France's most prominent artists and writers, including Gounod, Dumas *fils* and Maupassant, had led a fight against its construction. If the 1889 exposition, which had feted the centenary of the revolution, had been a huge success, the latest universal fair was still more fabulous. Ten years in the making, it transformed the city into a fantastical Venice of electric fountains and exhibition halls marvelously camouflaged with plaster palace fronts.

The Eiffel Tower and exposition grounds, Paris Exposition, 1900. By H. C. White.

Three Empires

Tsar Nicholas II, with the Tsaritsa Alexandra Feodorovna (to his right) and members of the imperial family, St. Petersburg, c. 1896. By B. W. Kilburn.

They were the world's three largest empires—which would, a few decades into the new century, belong to the ages. On June 22, 1897, at Queen Victoria's Diamond Jubilee, the British Empire was at its zenith. Fifty years later, on New Year's Eve, 1947, a socialist don occupying 10 Downing Street would preside over the dismemberment of the empire by extending freedom to India. For Tsarist Russia, its imperial days ended abruptly two decades after the coronation of Nicholas II. For China, the monarcho-bureaucratic system that had held the country together for 2,000 years ceased to exist in 1911, and it was left to Li Hung-chang—one of the few Chinese officials who saw the uses of Western technology in fighting off the foreign aggressors —to sign the treaties that reduced imperial China to a semi-colony.

Queen Victoria at breakfast with Princess Henry of Battenberg, her youngest daughter, and Princess Helena Victoria of Schleswig-Holstein (facing camera), a granddaughter, in Nice, April 1895. Standing behind them is Indian attendant Chidda. By Alexander Henderson.

Li Hung-chang, Chinese statesman and diplomat, 1900.

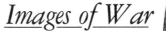

Images of War

*President Roosevelt
on the stump. By Underwood and Underwood.*

*Rough Riders saluting President McKinley in a reception in Los Angeles, 1901.
By Underwood and Underwood.*

It was a war demanded by the yellow journals, notably Hearst's *New York Journal;* those dreaming of an American empire to rival Britain's; and Theodore Roosevelt, the brash Assistant Secretary of the Navy in the McKinley Administration who supported annexation of Hawaii, Samoa, Cuba, and whatever else was available. And so, even as Madrid acceded to American demands to cease hostilities against the Cuban rebels, McKinley declared war on Spain in April 1898. Resigning from the Navy Department, Roosevelt led his Rough Riders in the battle of San Juan Hill and became an instant American hero. (Shortly thereafter he was drafted for the Vice Presidency.) The "splendid little war" that lasted 100 days ended America's long-held tradition against colonies and noncontiguous expansion. Two months into the war, Hawaii was annexed.

An American soldier guarding a prisoner, Spanish-American War, Cuba.

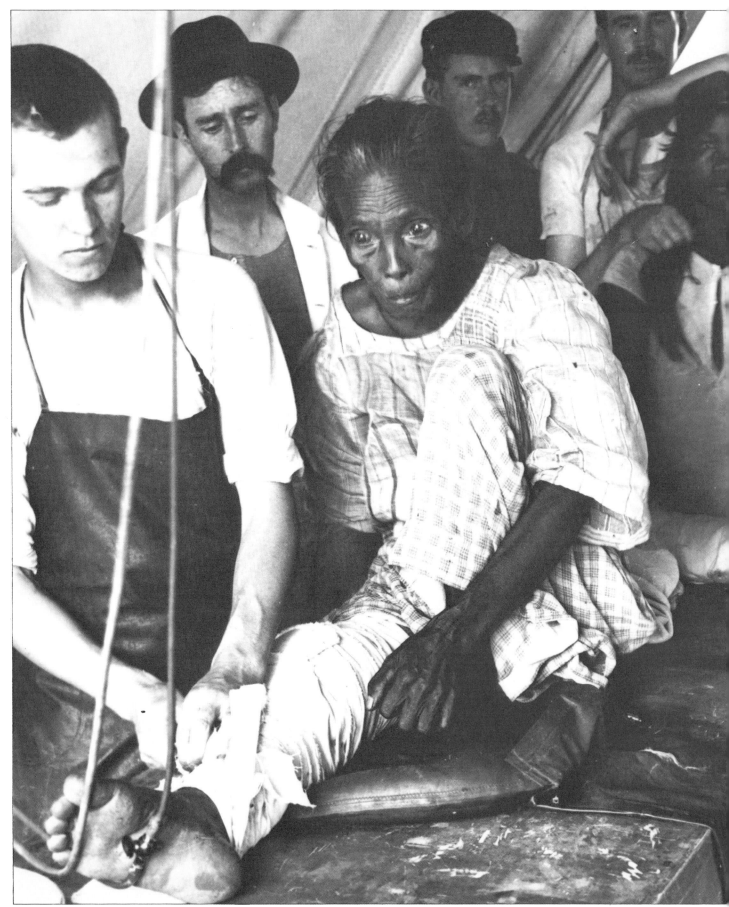

An old woman who was shot through the leg while carrying ammunition to the insurgents, Manila hospital.
By R. Y. Young of the American Stereoscopic Company.

Birth of the Cuban Republic, May 20, 1902, Governor-General's palace, Havana. By Underwood and Underwood.

While the Spanish-American War gave independence to Cuba, it turned Puerto Rico, Guam and the Philippine Islands into American colonies. Less than 400 miles from the China coast, the Philippines were deemed an ideal base from which American interests in China could be defended. But in order to acquire these islands as a colony, the United States had to put down a revolt for independence begun by the Filipinos two years before the start of the Spanish-American War. In February 1899, the United States started its campaign against the Filipino *insurrectos*. Lasting three and a half years, the war cost 4,000 Americans their lives. Because the rebels clearly had wide support, General J. M. Bell came to the conclusion that the only way to combat such a population was "to make the state of war as insupportable as possible." Soon, American soldiers were torturing and killing wounded enemy soldiers as well as unarmed civilians. Concentration camps were introduced. By General Bell's estimate, in Luzon alone about 100,-000 people were wiped out.

Execution chamber and garrote, Manila, 1899. By C. H. Graves.

British infantry fording the Vet River in its advance on Pretoria, March 1900. By Underwood and Underwood.

Boer farmers and boys on their way to the front, South Africa. By B. W. Kilburn.

The two-and-a-half-year Boer War, which began in October 1899, took 22,000 British lives and the lives of 25,000 Boers and 12,000 unfortunate Africans caught in the cross fire. Rudyard Kipling, who had believed in the invincibility of the British Empire and its role in shouldering the White Man's Burden, was appalled to find the army of *Pax Britannica* hard-pressed by desperate farmers who could ride and shoot. Britain won the war, but not before resorting to such tactics as the virtual imprisonment of the noncombatant inhabitants of the Transvaal (and of its ally, the Orange Free State) in concentration camps, where the death rate was shocking. Lord Kitchener also instituted the policy of laying waste the area of operations.

A British doctor operating on a wounded soldier, Boer War. By B. W. Kilburn.

Execution of a Boxer leader, China, 1900. By B. W. Kilburn.

Boxers guarded by Italian soldiers. By B. W. Kilburn.

In the early months of 1900, members of the *I-ho tuan* ("Righteous and Harmonious Society"), or Boxers, swept across North China, bent on the destruction of everything foreign. On June 20, they stormed into Peking, laying siege to the eleven foreign legations. The siege lasted fifty-five days, the Chinese Government meanwhile ignoring the foreigners' pleas for protection. Finally, on August 14, an expeditionary force of troops from the United States, Britain, France, Germany, Russia and Japan captured Peking, routed the Boxers and looted the city. The Western powers and Japan forthwith exacted from China the staggering indemnity of $333 million.

A band of insurgents, Greco-Turkish war, 1897. By Bert Underwood.

By the 19th century, the empire of the Ottoman Turks, founded in the 13th century, was the "sick man of Europe." Throughout the century, while the European balance of power simultaneously protected and dismembered Turkey, the empire's non-Turkish subjects waged their own wars of independence. Greece, which had fallen under Turkish rule in the 15th century, became independent in 1829, and thereafter sought to increase its territory. In 1897, following uprisings in Crete, which demanded union with Greece, Greek troops engaged in an unsuccessful war with Turkey, whose army had been undergoing reorganization under the Germans. Toward the end of the century, Palestine—which had become part of the Ottoman Empire in the 16th century—was seeing a weak Arab nationalism aimed at some form of local autonomy. At the same time, a group of Zionists was actively campaigning to establish a Jewish state in Palestine.

Bedouin robbers, wilderness of Judea, Palestine, 1896. By Bert Underwood.

Turkish military officers, Jerusalem, 1899. By B. W. Kilburn.

Outside stately Moscow and glittering, cosmopolitan St. Petersburg and a handful of other cities, the interminable Russian countryside remained much as it had for centuries. Here, according to the 1897 census, lived 87 percent of the population. Although Nicholas II's grandfather Alexander II had, in 1861, freed the country's serfs, life for the millions of peasants who had been the property of private landowners remained harsh and freedom virtually nonexistent.

Members of the royal families of Russia and Europe at the coronation of Tsar Nicholas II, 1896. Seated in the center are Grand Duchess Alexandra Iosifovna and the Duchess of Connaught (right), an aunt by marriage of the Tsaritsa Alexandra Feodorovna. By B. W. Kilburn.

Russian peasant families, c. 1896. By B. W. Kilburn.

*Ulysses S. Grant, U.S. soldier and 18th President
of the United States, with his wife, Julia, and youngest son,
Jesse, c. 1872. By G. W. Pach.*

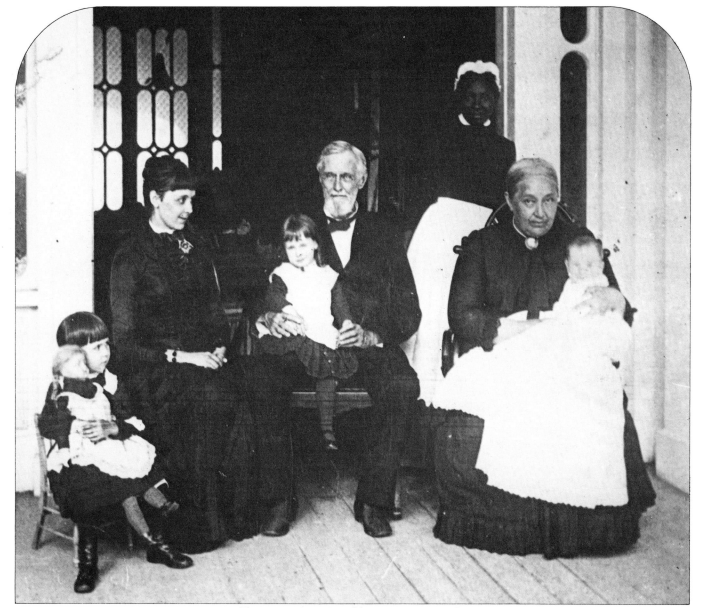

*Jefferson Davis, U.S. soldier, statesman and only
President of the Confederate States of America, with his wife, Varina,
daughter Maggie Hayes and her three children, c. 1885.*

*Lady Curzon, American heiress and wife of the
Viceroy of India, on the terrace of a bungalow in Kashmir, India.
By Underwood and Underwood.*

A frontier woman and her children at the Grand Canyon, Arizona.

A wealthy Cuban family. By Underwood and Underwood.

A peasant's home in Santiago de Cuba. By Underwood and Underwood.

Street Life

Left: Long-haired goats on a Swiss highway.

*Above: Candy vendors
in Kingston, Jamaica, 1899.
By C. H. Graves.*

*Right: Homeless beggars of Naples,
Italy. By H. C. White.*

*Below: Market scene in Warsaw, Poland,
c. 1896. By B. W. Kilburn.*

The Displaced

Geronimo, the Apache chief. By William H. Rau.

Convicts and their guards,
Atlanta, Georgia. By B. W. Kilburn.

Two Guns White Calf, the Blackfoot chief,
one of three models for the profile composite on the buffalo nickel.

Free to roam over nearly two billion acres of land and lakes for thousands of years, the American Indians at the end of the 19th century found themselves herded into an area that measured less than 3 percent of what was once their land. Shunted from one area of the country to another, told each time by the U.S. Government that the land they had would be theirs "in perpetuity" (and learning too late that "in perpetuity" meant "until gold or silver or copper or coal or oil is found, or settlers need farmland, or builders land for their railroad tracks"), the Indians compromised, they fought, they killed. But lacking the superior weaponry and the organizational skills of the "white fathers," the Indian nations were systematically decimated until, in December 1890 at Wounded Knee, Indian freedom came to a symbolic end. Among the South's blacks, the other major victims in the conquest of North America, many found themselves exchanging the shackles of slavery for the shackles of a chain gang. Until 1908, the majority of prisoners in Georgia were leased to private businesses or assigned to local chain gangs.

A Chinese woman and her children outside their cabin in Olympia, Washington. By B. W. Kilburn.

Between 1840 and 1920, the world saw its largest migration of peoples, many of whom crossed continents and oceans to settle in America. Beginning in 1892, immigrants from steerage class who entered the United States at the Port of New York were brought to Ellis Island, where examinations by officers of the Public Health and Immigration services would determine whether they could be admitted. (Those traveling in cabins were presumably of the "better" classes and did not require "weeding out.") Undesirables barred from admission included the mentally ill, epileptics, paupers, polygamists, anarchists and Chinese laborers. Although Chinese laborers had been welcome in the 1860s to build the first transcontinental railroad, once the work was done they were seen as a threat to white labor. Sinophobia, which first erupted in California mining towns in 1849, culminated in the Chinese Exclusion Act of 1882, America's first bill to restrict immigration on a racial basis.

Immigrants at Ellis Island undergoing examinations by Public Health officers. By Underwood and Underwood.

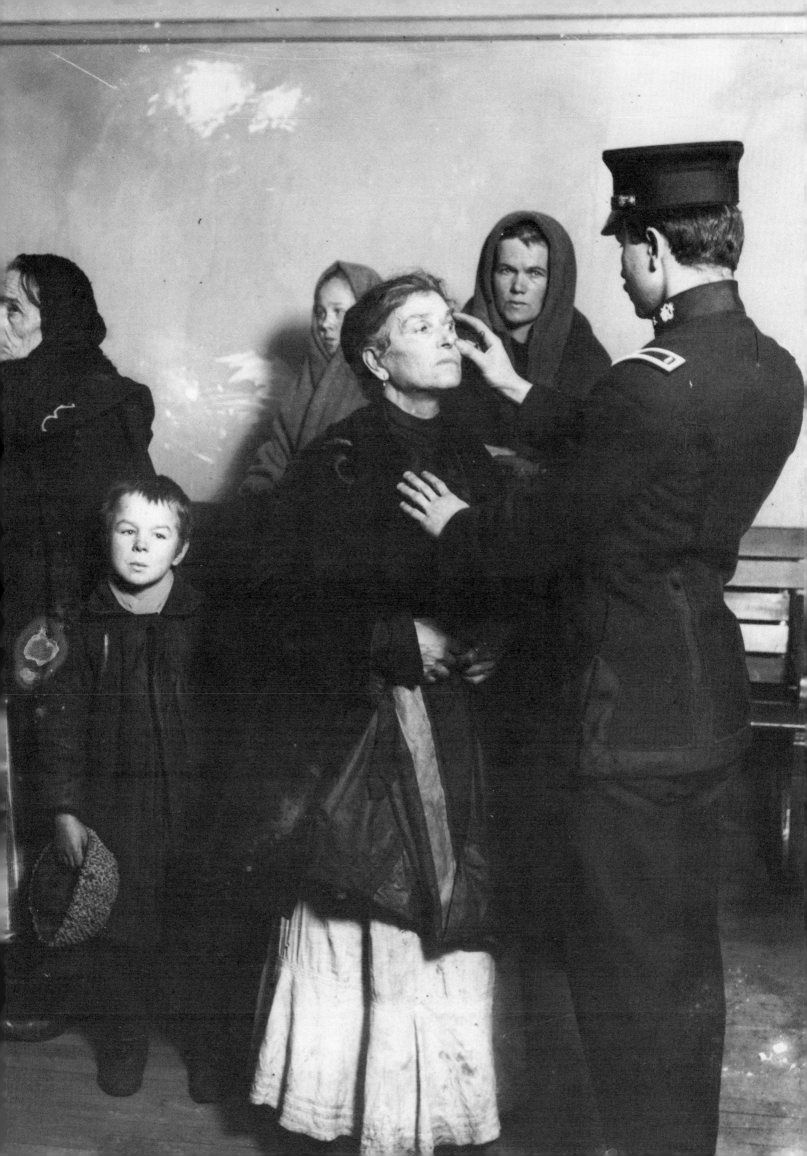

Three Writers

Right: Henry Wadsworth Longfellow in his study in Cambridge, Massachusetts, c. 1876.

Below: Henrik Ibsen in his home in Oslo, Norway. By Underwood and Underwood.

Facing page: Mark Twain in the billiard room of his house in Hartford, Connecticut. By Underwood and Underwood.

Simple Pleasures

Children in a Brussels park, Belgium.

The Acropolis and Likavittós from Philopappus Hill,
Athens, Greece. By Elmer Underwood.

65

An amusement park in Coburg, Germany.
By Underwood and Underwood.

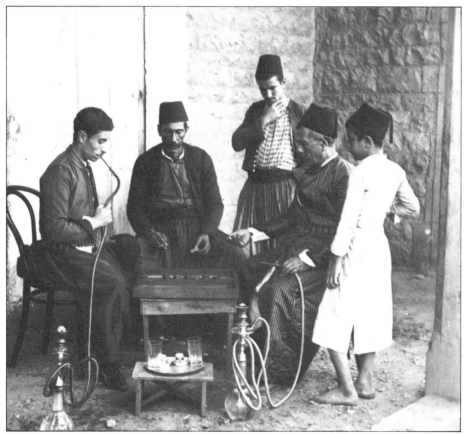

A game of Turkish backgammon in Palestine, 1900. By Keystone View Company.

Cossacks dancing, Russia, c. 1896. By B. W. Kilburn.

Atlantic City beach, New Jersey, 1891. By B. W. Kilburn.

Bicycle riding in the city, c. 1890s.
By Underwood and Underwood.

Interiors . . .

Left: Casino at Monte Carlo, Monaco.

Top: Salon of American Embassy, Russia. By C. H. Graves.

Right: The White Salon in the Winter Palace, St. Petersburg, Russia. By William H. Rau.

Below: Song Ying Lo, a chop suey house in Chicago, Illinois. By H. C. White.

Statue of Bismarck in front of the Reichstagsgebäude (Parliament Building),
Berlin, Germany. By H. C. White.

Home of a wealthy merchant in Moscow.

Russia. By H. C. White.

THE NEW YORK HERALD

New York Herald Building at Broadway and Thirty-fourth Street,

Water station in Moscow, Russia, c. 1896. By B. W. Kilburn.

Mounted warriors with chain armor and metal breastplates, Delhi, India.

The new century saw India and Africa in the hands of colonialists, and China having whole sections cut away at the outer rim. Under the British, there were actually two Indias: one ruled directly by the British, the other through rajas and maharajas, who had been created by Providence, it once seemed to Kipling, to offer mankind a spectacle of mythical opulence and medieval pageantry. China was hapless before a serious imperialist contender like Japan, which controlled Manchuria after the Russo-Japanese War, annexing Korea in 1910; Formosa had been ceded to it in 1895. Germany's "sphere of influence" was Shantung Province; France's, Kwangchow. In the 1890s, France had combined Annam, Cochin China (South Vietnam), Tonkin, Laos and Cambodia into French Indochina. Britain, which had annexed Burma in 1886, dominated the Yangtze Valley. In Africa, Germany established colonies in East Africa, in the Cameroons and Togo, and in South-West Africa. France controlled most of north and west Africa, and British influence stretched from the Union of South Africa and Rhodesia to Kenya, Uganda, British Somalia, the Sudan and Egypt.

Government officials and staff, Seoul, Korea. By Underwood and Underwood.

Vietnamese soldiers near a boat landing in Saigon, Cochin China. By James Ricalton of Underwood and Underwood.

A Chinese military officer and his bodyguards, China.

Natives of Uganda beside a mammoth rock, 1909. By Underwood and Underwood.

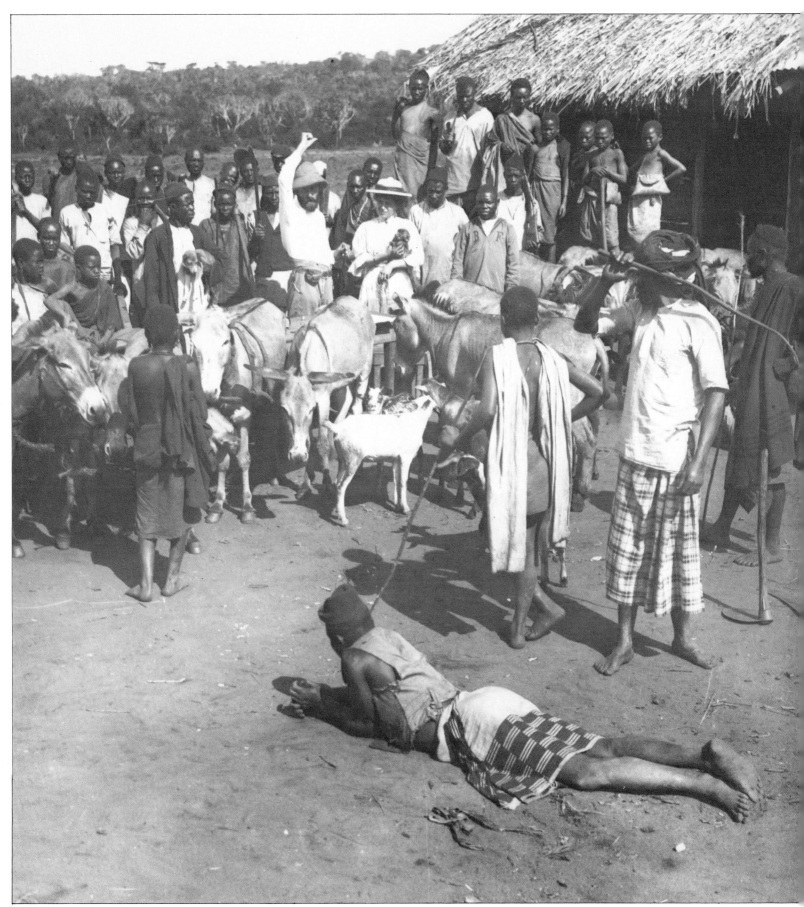

A German on a rubber plantation counting the strokes at a beating of a native, East Africa. By Underwood and Underwood.

Colombia was cool to the project of a canal through its province of Panama, and for a while it looked as though the United States would be building a Nicaragua canal. Quite fortuitously, a revolt broke out on November 3, 1903, in Panama, and with the American superintendent of the Panama Railroad seeing to it that no train was available to move Colombian troops there to put down the rebellion, independence was proclaimed. Three days later, the United States recognized the new republic and promptly signed a treaty authorizing construction of a canal that would cross the Isthmus of Panama from the Atlantic to the Pacific. On November 18, the United States acquired "perpetual" control of the Canal Zone, which basically cut the country in two. (On October 1, 1979, jurisdiction over the Canal Zone was transferred to Panama.) One of the world's greatest engineering feats, the Panama Canal was completed in 1914.

Work in progress at Gatun Locks. The pit dug was about a mile and a quarter long, 600 feet wide and about 50 feet deep.

Family Album

A Visayan family, Cebu, Philippines.

Mr. and Mrs. James Ward and family, Creggs, Ireland, 1905. By Underwood and Underwood.

Three generations, Pretoria, South Africa. By B. W. Kilburn.

A Chinese woman (background) with her maidservants, Hong Kong, c. 1901.
By James Ricalton of Underwood and Underwood.

An American couple. By Underwood and Underwood.

An Admiral of the River Fleet with his wife and daughter, China, c. 1901.
By James Ricalton of Underwood and Underwood.

Maori mothers with their babies, New Zealand.

Fathers and sons, the Congo. By Underwood and Underwood.

The Ainus of Japan, 1906. By H. C. White.

A Korean couple, Seoul, 1904. By Underwood and Underwood.

A bride and groom with their attendants halting by the wayside en route to the wedding, Japan, 1906. By Keystone View Company.

A Norwegian family. By T. W. Ingersoll.

A fisherman and his family, Island of Markham, the Netherlands.
By Underwood and Underwood.

A Jamaican couple.

A woman and her daughters,
Bretton Woods, New Hampshire.
By Underwood and Underwood.

An Algerian home. By Underwood and Underwood.

A Salish family of western Montana, 1907. By Underwood and Underwood.

Two Sinai women and their children. By Underwood and Underwood.

Luna Park, Coney Island, by day. By Underwood and Underwood.

Leisure Moments

At night, Luna Park's red-and-white minarets and towers with their cupolas, domes and archways silhouetted by 250,000 electric lights overwhelmed even the brooding Russian novelist Maxim Gorky. "Thousands of ruddy sparks glimmer in the darkness," he wrote, "limning in fine, sensitive outline on the black background of the sky shapely towers of miraculous castles, palaces and temples. . . . Fabulous beyond conceiving, ineffably beautiful, is this fiery scintillation." Opened in 1903, the sprawling 32-acre park was packed with rides (including shoot-the-chutes, a ride in a flat-bottomed boat down a watered incline to a lagoon), a three-ring circus, shooting galleries, and such spectacles as four elephants sliding down a special shoot-the-chutes. In 1945, Luna Park, Gorky's "fantastic city all of fire," burned to the ground.

Luna Park by night. By Underwood and Underwood.

Yun Wong-Niel, Korean Minister of War (left),
in a game of Go with a friend in his home in Seoul, Korea, 1904.
By Underwood and Underwood.

Women playing dominoes, Palm Beach, Florida. By Underwood and Underwood.

A crowd gathered around
an American phonograph
in a Tokyo park, 1906.
By H. C. White.

Tokyo fine-arts class.

Sculptor at work, Acropolis Museum, Athens, Greece.
By Underwood and Underwood.

Women fencers, Japan.

A zoo keeper and his laughing monkey, 1907.
By H. C. White.

A child afloat on a victoria regia,
Como Park, St. Paul, Minnesota.
By Underwood and Underwood.

Children playing Blindman's Buff.

Peking Mission School children at play, China, 1902. By C. H. Graves.

Faces of Labor

Silk-weaving plant, Kiryu, Japan.

A woman spinning silk from cocoons, Japan.

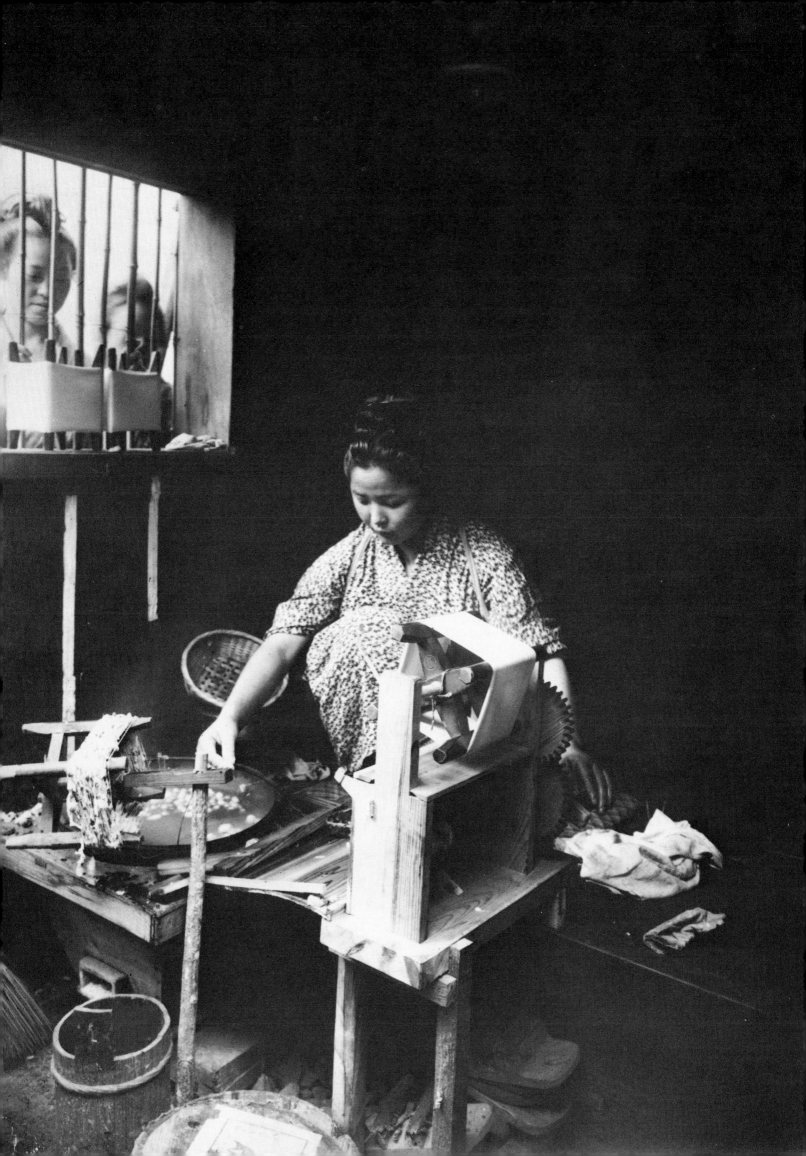

A woman and her children ironing clothes, Island of Luzon, Philippines.

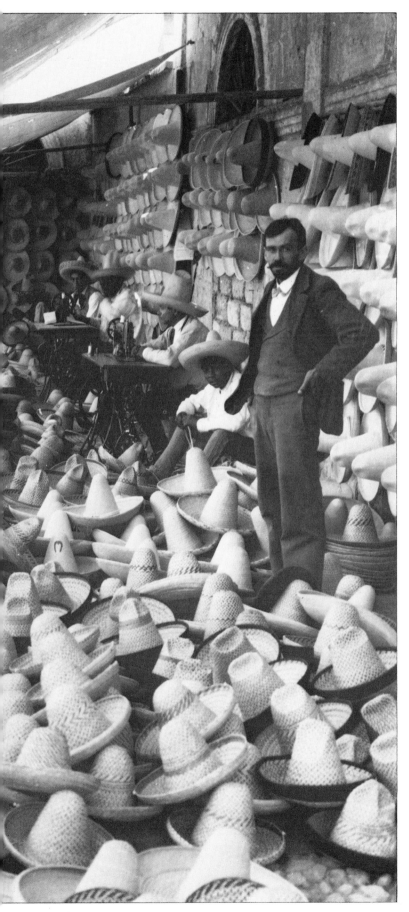

A toy seller's stock, Tokyo, Japan, 1906. By H. C. White.

A sombrero store, Mexico City, Mexico, 1903.
By Underwood and Underwood.

*Above: A schoolboy giving a contribution
to an itinerant Buddhist priest who carries on his back a portable altar
equipped with his religious paraphernalia, Japan.*

*Right: A bamboo-basket seller sharing a joke with his customer,
Japan, 1904. By Keystone View Company.*

Below: A street barber, Peking, China, 1902. By C. H. Graves.

A fruit seller, Jaipur, India, 1902. By Keystone View Company.

Medicines offered by a Bhutanese woman, Darjeeling, India, 1903. By Underwood and Underwood.

A lemonade vendor and his customer, Cairo, Egypt. By B. W. Kilburn.

*A woman carrying a bucket of grapes on her head,
Rüdesheim, Germany, 1905. By Keystone View Company.*

*Right: Working at the salt mines, San Fernando,
Spain. By Underwood and Underwood.*

Women sorting coffee beans, Nicaragua, 1902.

*Zebra hunting in Tanganyika Territory, Africa.
By Underwood and Underwood.*

*Elephant tusks ready for shipment to New York,
Mombasa, Kenya, 1909. By Underwood and Underwood.*

After a day's hunt in the Yangtze River Valley, China.

Boatmen inflating bullock-skin boats, Sutlej River, India, 1903. By Underwood and Underwood.

Africans beside a crocodile that was shot by a white hunter, Uganda, 1909. By Underwood and Underwood.

Artisans restoring an old Persian rug, Constantinople, Turkey, 1912. By Underwood and Underwood.

Craftsmen making bronze lanterns for a temple, Kyoto, Japan, 1907. By H. C. White.

A woman at the spinning wheel, India. By B. W. Kilburn.

*Laborers transporting pots
to the interior, Chosan, Korea.
By B. W. Kilburn.*

Irish peasant women carrying peat, Ireland, 1903. By William H. Rau.

Men with bundles of hay,
Simla, India, 1903.
By Underwood and Underwood.

Men working at a quartz-sorting table,
Robinson Mine, Johannesburg, South Africa.

Excavating for gold ore, Village Deep Gold Mines,
South Africa. By Underwood and Underwood.

Blacks picking cotton in Texas.

Placer mining near the Yukon River, Alaska.

Portuguese peasants standing below Pena Castle in Sintra, Portugal.
By Underwood and Underwood.

Fishermen mending nets, Hastings, England.
By Underwood and Underwood.

A twenty-woman team working on a highway, Darjeeling, India, 1903. By Underwood and Underwood.

The Schoolroom

Day nursery, 1907. Brown Bros.

145

The Daisy Chain carried by sophomores ushering out the year's graduating class, Commencement Day, Vassar College, Poughkeepsie, New York, c. 1906. By Underwood and Underwood.

The first country to provide universal education through a public school system, the United States since the 1850s had seen states pass compulsory-attendance laws; by 1918 all states had some requirements for attendance at school, even though, after the Civil War, segregated school systems for black and white children had been established in the Southern states and the District of Columbia. By the 1880s, primary-school education was compulsory in France, Britain, Germany and Japan. Throughout much of the world, education for girls lagged far behind that of boys; in Prussia, for instance, secondary schools for girls had been dealt with administratively as part of the elementary-school system. It wasn't until 1908 that women were admitted to German universities on the same terms as men.

Booker T. Washington, founder of Tuskegee Institute, and family, 1905. Underwood and Underwood.

Gym class, Tuskegee Institute, Alabama, 1905. By Underwood and Underwood.

Hessian schoolgirls in their holiday costume, Mengsburg, near Treysa, Germany, 1908. By Underwood and Underwood.

Children in Warsaw, Poland. By B. W. Kilburn.

Above: Chinese schoolchildren
and their teacher at an American
Board of Missions school, Peking. By
Keystone View Company.

Left: Jamaican schoolchildren
and their teacher, Jamaica, 1904.
By H. C. White.

Below: At a mission school for girls,
Lydda, Palestine. By Underwood
and Underwood.

Right: A schoolmaster and his pupil,
Monaghan County, Ireland. By
Underwood and Underwood.

The Great Outdoors

Attracted by reports of a fertile valley and grants of free land from
the government, thousands in the 1840s traveled in covered wagons
along the 2,000-mile Oregon Trail from Independence, Missouri, to
the Columbia River country of Oregon. A half-century later, with
the Oklahoma territory officially settled, and with no line left
dividing open frontier from "civilization," the United States Bureau
of the Census declared the frontier closed. This stereograph by
H. C. White was taken on the great sand dunes along
the Columbia River, Oregon.

The Louisiana Purchase Exposition, St. Louis, Missouri, 1904. By H. C. White.

154

Exposition park, Louisiana Purchase Exposition, St. Louis, Missouri. By Underwood and Underwood.

At the edge of the crater of Asosan, central Kyushu, Japan, 1906.
By H. C. White.

The eruption of Mount Pelée, Martinique, 1902.

Two girls on the bridge across the River Ouse, near Ely, England, 1911. By Underwood and Underwood.

Lake Louise and the glacier of Mount Victoria, Alberta, Canada.

Niagara Falls, New York. By Underwood and Underwood.

Princes Street, Edinburgh, Scotland. By Underwood and Underwood.

Medieval gateway to the town of Lübeck, Germany.
By Underwood and Underwood.

A hammock carriage, Funchal, Madeira. By Underwood and Underwood.

One-wheeled cart of a Korean general,
Seoul, Korea, 1904.
By Underwood and Underwood.

A woman carried in a palanquin,
Botanical Gardens, Darjeeling, India. By Underwood and Underwood.

A palanquin in Calcutta, India.
By Underwood and Underwood.

Above: The Opera House, Paris, c. *1901.*
By Underwood and Underwood.

Right: Ezra Meeker with the wagon and ox team he drove
across the continent to promote the commemorative marking of the Oregon Trail,
through which he had traveled in the 1850s;
New York City, 1907. By Underwood and Underwood.

Below: "Joan of Arc" among the suffragists, coronation procession,
London, 1911. By Underwood and Underwood.

Street scene, Bakuba village, the Congo, Africa. By Underwood and Underwood.

A street in the Arab quarter of Algiers, Algeria. By C. H. Graves.

Naples, Italy. By H. C. White.

Genoa, Italy. By H. C. White.

The San Francisco Earthquake

*A woman
camping by the roadside.
By H. C. White.*

*Cable cars demolished by the disaster, stored east of Hyde Street on
California. By Underwood and Underwood.*

At 5:12 A.M. on April 18, 1906, when most of the people in San Francisco were still asleep, the earth opened up and a deafening roar filled the quiet city. Even as the ground heaved, fires were ignited which quickly spread through thousands of wood-frame buildings. When it was all over, 450 people had been killed and most of the city's central business and residential districts demolished, the estimated damage totaling $500 million.

Bank vaults cracked during the earthquake, their contents gutted by fire. By Underwood and Underwood.

A monument destroyed by the earthquake. By Underwood and Underwood.

171

The Flying Machine

Along a sandy strip of beach in
Kitty Hawk, North Carolina, two brothers on
December 17, 1903, did the impossible.
Admittedly, the first flight on their motor-driven,
heavier-than-air contraption lasted twelve
seconds, but for the first time, a machine carrying
a man "had raised itself by its own power into
the air in full flight," Orville Wright later recounted,
"had sailed forward without reduction of speed,
and had finally landed at a point as high as that from
which it started." On the fourth flight that day,
Wilbur Wright kept his airplane flying for fifty-nine
seconds. Two years later, the singular achievement
of the Wright brothers was still met with
skepticism and even scorn. The magazine *Scientific
American*, for one, referred to the "alleged"
flights. Worldwide attention was finally focused on
the brothers in 1908 when Wilbur set a new
record in France by circling high in the air
for one hour and fifty-four minutes. Wilbur died of
typhoid fever in 1912. A month after Orville's
death in January 1948, a jet fighter plane
flew the 950 miles from Seattle to Los Angeles
in one hour and fifty-eight minutes.

*Wilbur Wright flying
over Governors Island, New York,
at 45 miles an hour, 1909.
By H. C. White.*

Indoors

Amber Palace, India. By B. W. Kilburn.

The great durbar hall in the palace of the Maharaja of Gwalior, India. By Underwood and Underwood.

Main library of the University of Prague, Czechoslovakia.

A monastery, Portugal. By Underwood and Underwood.

Portraits

Wa-Kikuyu women and young girl, highlanders of south-central Kenya. By Underwood and Underwood.

Wa-Kikuyu spearmen. By Underwood and Underwood.

*A sumo wrestler and a child, Japan. By James Ricalton of
Underwood and Underwood.*

Sheik el-Sadaat, Egypt, 1910.

Ali bin Hamed bin Mohammed, Sultan of Zanzibar and Pemba.

A woman of Zanzibar holding a suni.
By Underwood and Underwood.

A woman of New York City, 1909.
By Underwood and Underwood.

An old woman of Seattle, Washington. By B. W. Kilburn.

A woman of Guadeloupe, West Indies.

Left: Officials of Kandy, Ceylon. By Underwood and Underwood.

Above: Shan chiefs from Burma at the Great Durbar
of 1903 held in honor of Edward VII's coronation, Delhi, India.
By Underwood and Underwood.

Above, right: Famine victims receiving aid, India, c. 1901.
By Keystone View Company.

Right: A man on a bed of nails, India, 1907. By H. C. White.

Left: Pastoral Masai women with their shaven heads and clothes of dressed skins, Kenya. By Underwood and Underwood.

Right: A chief, wearing a necklace of leopards' teeth, with two retainers and an interpreter visiting Basoko, the Belgian Congo. By Underwood and Underwood.

A warrior of New Guinea.

Aboriginal huntsmen with their boomerangs, Healesville, Victoria, Australia. By Underwood and Underwood.

A group of Manchu noblewomen and a maidservant,
Peking, China, 1902. By C. H. Graves.

Women of Tehuantepec, Oaxaca, Mexico. By Underwood and Underwood.

Lepers begging outside the walls of Jerusalem. By H. C. White.

The Samaritans, Palestine. By B. W. Kilburn.

A Russian couple at a hospice, Jerusalem, Palestine.
By Underwood and Underwood.

PART III

THE END OF AN AGE
1914–1921

"You will be home before the leaves have fallen from the trees," the Kaiser told his departing troops the first week of August 1914.

In Whitehall the evening of August 3, Sir Edward Grey, Britain's Prime Minister, stood with a friend at a window as the street lamps below were being lit and remarked, "The lamps are going out all over Europe; we shall not see them lit again in our lifetime."

•

In the Great War, the 19th and 20th centuries met for the last time and parted forever.

With all the panache of a fin-de-siècle aesthete, General Edmund Allenby, ordered in June 1917 to safeguard the inviolability of the Suez Canal by capturing all of the Sinai, all of Palestine and as much of the rest of the Levant as he could, rode through the desert in an open command car, bird-watching along the way and having a French chef prepare his meals in the field.

Uniforms for the troops ranged from nondescript modern utilitarian to showy 19th-century dash. After the Boer War, the British had switched to khaki uniforms. The Germans had replaced Prussian blue with field-gray uniforms; the cavalry, however, rode— like some medieval horsemen—with black and white pennants fluttering from their lances, and cavalry officers were observed to be partial to monocles and English riding crops.

Over the protests of Adolphe Messimy, the Minister of War, the French soldiers went to war conspicuously attired in the blue coats, red kepis and red trousers they had worn in 1830 when rifles had a range of 200 paces and there had not been a need for concealment. (Officers from St. Cyr rode into battle wearing white-plumed shakos and white gloves.) To their everlasting regret, the French generals were no more willing to dress the French soldier in some drab, inglorious color than they were to accept heavy field artillery as a crucial weapon of war.

The Scottish regiments, similarly ill-attired in their kilts, suffered through the winter of 1916–17, one of the coldest in Europe in decades.

With motor vehicles at a premium, magnificent limousines were pressed into service as transports. In September 1914, General Joseph-Simon Gallieni used 1,200 Paris taxicabs to rush every available man to fight the Germans at the river Marne. Machines of war were transported by railway and hurried to the battlefield by every available means. In Belgium, machine guns were pulled, like the milk carts of Flanders, by dogs.

Modern armies had become extraordinarily large, but the necessary means of communicating under war conditions had not been fully developed. Since the wireless radio was still in its infancy, the command staffs had to depend on such unmodern means as runners, dogs and carrier pigeons for military communications.

Notwithstanding the dispatching of military observers to the Russo-Japanese war, none of the belligerents, including Russia, understood the mechanics of modern warfare. Many of the generals had never directed large formations in *la grande guerre,* and they went to war juxtaposing 19th-century assault tactics with 20th-century weaponry—a cruel juxtaposition that led to the appalling carnage at the Marne, the Somme, Verdun, Passchendaele, Ypres and Flanders Field.

In learning the tactics of assault, French infantrymen had been taught that they could cover 50 meters in 20 seconds—the time needed for the enemy infantry to shoulder guns, take aim and fire. On the battlefield, German machine guns, requiring only eight seconds to fire, tore gaping holes in the French ranks. At the beginning of the war, only the Germans realized the power of the weapon of the machine age—the machine gun. The Germans had 4,500 machine guns, compared with the 2,500 of the French; the British had fewer than 500.

The new artillery weapons could be worked behind armored shields and fired as quickly as 20 times a minute; the replacement of black powder with a smokeless kind allowed the gunners to see their targets throughout an artillery attack; rifled artillery shells had a spin that increased the range and accuracy of shellfire.

Since the new weapons were astonishingly effective weapons of defense, each side built a line of defensive trenches to keep the other side from breaking through. By the end of 1914, a gigantic gash was cut across the face of Europe from the North Sea to the Alps.

As the war dragged on, year after year, newer and more formidable weapons were devised and used in the hope they would end the horrifying trench warfare. Huge naval guns, intended for use on battleships, were mounted on railway cars and sent to the battlefield, where they flung shells each weighing a ton or more at targets invisible to the gunners. Aircraft, which started as "flying eyes" for the army, became fighter planes. The first British heavy bombers flew at 60 to 80 miles an hour and could carry a bomb load of 1,800 pounds. German Zeppelins dropped bombs. Howitzers and mortars were refined for deadly accuracy. Shrapnel shells showered hundreds of metal projectiles on the enemy; shells holding poison gases killed or blinded.

Tanks, first developed by the British for this war, could have been used to break the trench stalemate, but their effectiveness was discounted until the end of the war. Lord Kitchener, Minister of War, called the tank a "pretty, mechanical toy . . . the war will never be won by such machines."

To counter the British blockade that was slowly starving Germany into submission, the Germans were the first to deploy modern submarines in sizable numbers. But it was the torpedoing of the liner *Lusitania,* with 128 Americans on board, that led in part to the entry of the United States into the war.

•

In one four-year war, four empires fell.

The first to fall, before the war ended, was the Russian Empire. From August 1914 through the long winter of 1916–17, the armies of mainly peasant conscripts, poorly trained, poorly armed and poorly commanded, lost men by the millions. Finally, in March 1917, the people of St. Petersburg revolted. Cold, weary, hungry, they began demonstrating as they queued for bread. The disturbances spread throughout the city. The troops ordered to suppress the near riots joined the demonstrators; these were rear-area soldiers, not the Guards regiments, which were now at the front. On March 15 Nicholas II abdicated, and a provisional government was formed. But, believing that it could succeed as a liberal and parliamentary regime if the German Empire was defeated, the new government waged the war even more vigorously with the same limited resources. In July 1917, in an offensive in Galicia, the demoralized Russian armies collapsed. Hoping to capitalize on the turmoil in Russia, Germany a few months earlier had offered Vladimir Ilyich Lenin, who was then living in exile in Switzerland, safe passage home through Germany. In the confusion of November 1917, Lenin and the Bolsheviks seized power and proclaimed the world's first socialist country.

A defeated Germany, stripped of all its colonies as well as territories within the former empire claimed by the French, the Poles and the Lithuanians, became the Weimar Republic.

Austria and Hungary were now small states; Turkey, confined to Constantinople and Asia Minor, was a small republic.

Seven new independent states emerged: Finland, Estonia, Latvia, Lithuania, Poland, Czechoslovakia and Yugoslavia.

The victorious Allies continued—with the exception of the United States—their brazen prewar practices of territorial expansion. (The United States Senate, in a wave of isolationism and disgust with Europe, refused to ratify the Treaty of Versailles or permit the United States to join the League of Nations.) Syria and Lebanon were bestowed on France as mandates of the League of Nations; Palestine and Iraq on Britain, under the same terms. France and Britain took the best of Germany's African colonies; the Union of South Africa took over German South-West Africa. Japan received the mandate for the German Pacific islands north of the equator; Australia, for German New Guinea and the Solomon Islands; New Zealand, for German Samoa. Japan, despite the protests of the Chinese delegation to the Versailles Peace Conference, also claimed the rights to the German concessions in China. (The Chinese were equally unsuccessful in getting the powers to abolish all special concessions and extraterritorial rights in China.)

But while the behavior of Britain and France at the conference table differed little from their prewar imperialistic behavior, they, and the rest of Europe, victor or vanquished, had been severely crippled by the war. Total deaths on the Western Front for Britain

were 700,000; France, 1.3 million; Germany, 1.2 million. The war had cost Britain $35 million a day; for France, the budget for the war amounted to 125 billion francs (the budget for the whole of 1913 was 5 billion francs); in Germany, the cost of the war had risen to $32 million a day by 1918. Creditors to the world before 1914, all three were now debtor nations, with the United States assuming Britain's former role of major creditor to the world.

To cover their huge wartime budget deficits, governments printed more money, sold more bond issues, took out more loans. With a heavy postwar demand and acute shortages, the world saw its first large-scale inflation, which reached epidemic proportions in Eastern and Central Europe and particularly in Germany. In 1914 there were 20 German marks to the pound sterling; the rate rose to 250 in 1920, climbed to 1,000 in 1921 and soared to 35,000 in 1922. The hardest hit were those with fixed incomes, the professional people, government employees—namely, the middle class, which had been a stabilizing influence in prewar Europe.

Europe ceased to be the world's workshop. During the war, the rest of the world speeded up its industrialization, especially the United States and Japan. The Japanese quickly took the place of Britain in supplying cotton textiles and other civilian goods to China, India and South America. Unable to get locomotive parts or mining machinery from Britain, Argentina and Brazil began to manufacture their own. India developed one of the largest iron and steel works in the British Empire.

If the 19th-century economic foundations of Europe were undermined by the war, the social foundations of the postwar world were shaken to the core. Men and women were unwilling to return to the pre-1914 society in which people were stratified by class and sex. In the trenches, millions of soldiers had shared a rough equality with the officers, men whose birth, schooling and social standing had traditionally kept them apart from the "lower classes."

During the war, women flocked to factories and offices, many taking over jobs that were once known as "men's work." When the war ended, these women—from the lower to the upper classes—could no longer return to a life of servitude or one of ceremonial futility. More than anything else, the war put to rest this prevalent prewar notion reported by Thorstein Veblen in *The Theory of the Leisure Class* (1899): "It is unfeminine in [a woman] to aspire to a self-directing, self-centered life; and our common sense tells us that her direct participation in the affairs of the community, civil or industrial, is a menace to that social order which expresses our habits of thought as they have been formed under the guidance of the traditions of the pecuniary culture."

Governments in postwar Europe and America for a moment resolved the "woman question" by giving women the vote (in some countries suffrage was qualified, in others not). Between 1917 and 1919, women's suffrage was adopted in Britain, the United States, Russia, Austria, Czechoslovakia, Germany, Hungary, Poland, Canada, British East Africa, Ireland, Rhodesia, Scotland, Wales, Belgium, Holland, Iceland, Luxembourg and Sweden. While Finland had extended the vote to women in 1906 and Norway in 1913, before 1900 women could vote only in Australia, New Zealand and the American states of Wyoming, Colorado, Idaho and Utah.

.

After the war, the three largest scrambling grounds of the great powers—China, India and Africa—were caught up in furious nationalistic movements that eventually freed them from foreign domination. Yet in all these territories, peace—which independence and the war to end all wars had promised—was illusory. The dragon's teeth of 19th-century imperialism had been sown, which future generations of Chinese, Indians and Africans were to reap.

During the war, China for the first time faced a new threat: outright colonization. After the outbreak of war, Japan, as an ally of Britain, took control of German colonies and concessions in the Far East, including Yap, in the Carolines, and the German sphere of influence in the Chinese province of Shantung. In January 1915, Japan secretly presented to the Republic of China the infamous Twenty-one Demands, acceptance of which would have reduced China to the status of a Japanese colony. The Chinese Government, seeing it was in its best interest to leak out the contents of the demands, won the intervention of the Western powers.

If they were beset without by a rapacious Japan, the Chinese were beset within by rapacious warlords, who warred on each other, organized the opium trade, sold official posts, extorted from merchants and peasants alike.

Yet while the warlords spread like a cancer across the land, a new nationalism was catching the imagination of the country's students, scholars and workers. When the news reached Peking at the end of April 1919 that the Versailles Peace Conference had failed to end Japanese and Western overlordship in China, huge student demonstrations were held in Peking on May 4, 1919; among their leaders was a 21-year-old student, Chou En-lai. What became known as the May Fourth Movement marked the beginning of China's Second Revolution, which had as its objectives the ousting of all foreign imperialists and the replacement of ancient values and ideas with those better suited to meet the challenges of a modern world. Toward that end, scholars pressed for the acceptance of vernacular Chinese, then known as the "vulgar tongue of the people." Other than cheap novels, which appeared in the vernacular, all books were written in classical Chinese, which was far too esoteric for the average person to read. Feeling that it was  patently absurd to try to build a popular movement and spread new ideas if the common person on the street could not read, leaders of the cultural revolution flooded the country with magazines, newspapers and books printed in the vernacular. By 1920 the vernacular had become the accepted written language of China.

Convinced now that only a country united in a common purpose could bring about a new China, intellectuals—who had traditionally remained aloof from the "common people"—established contacts with merchants, industrialists, urban workers and the peasants in the countryside.

When "democracy" as it had appeared to the Chinese people proved to be a false god, intellectuals looked to the October Revolution in Russia as a possible solution to China's problems. Groups of Marxists formed in the large cities. In July 1921 the Chinese Communist Party was founded in Shanghai; among the founders was a 28-year-old Hunanese named Mao Tse-tung.

•

When the Great War ended, Mohandas Karamchand Gandhi—the world's unlikeliest revolutionary—had been leading his people in nonviolent noncooperation for over a decade. It had started in 1907 when he was a young lawyer in South Africa. That year, the Government passed a law that would have forced Indians over the age of eight to register with the Government, be fingerprinted and carry special identity cards. Gandhi quickly organized a passive-resistance campaign, which became known as *Satyagraha* ("truth force"). Six years later, when South Africa's Supreme Court ruled that "Hindu, Muslim and Parsee marriages were invalid, therefore Indian wives were concubines without status, liable to deportation, and the children were illegitimate," Gandhi led a mass march, filling the jails with his followers. But even before the Government had to contend with outside censure, it capitulated and met Gandhi's demands, including the recognition of non-Christian marriages and the mitigation of immigration and residence regulations.

The India that Gandhi saw after his return from South Africa in 1915 was not the India of 1877, when Queen Victoria was proclaimed Empress of India. Indian literature had been carried to the world when the poet Rabindranath Tagore won the Nobel Prize in 1913. During the war, the Tata family's Iron and Steel Company became one of the largest iron and steel works in the British Empire. The fall of the Tsar in Russia had a profound impact on India (if a mighty autocracy like the Russian Empire could fall, so too could India's), as had President Wilson's Fourteen Points, which recognized the right to self-determination of all nations.

Now in February 1919, when the British Government of India, feeling the country's discontent, enacted the Rowlatt Bills, which gave the colonial authorities the power to imprison without trial anyone suspected of sedition, Gandhi called on the people in the cities to observe a *hartal,* or stoppage of work on the grounds of conscience. When Gandhi was arrested, crowds rioted. In April 1919, British troops fired on a crowd without warning and, according to official reports, killed 379 and wounded 1,200.

Under the leadership of Mahatma ("Great Soul") Gandhi, India embarked on a quarter-century of nonviolent civil disobedience that was to bring down the most powerful empire on earth.

•

With the outbreak of the Great War for Civilization in Europe, Africans were pitched willy-nilly into a white man's war.

From August 1914, Africa was second only to Europe as a battlefield (the most celebrated German missionary taken prisoner by his French colleagues was Albert Schweitzer). In East Africa, which, with an area of 384,000 square miles, was the largest of Germany's African possessions, the fighting lasted as long as the warfare in Europe. Germany's East African army started with 5,000 troops, 260 of them Europeans. For their East African campaign, the Allies had in their armies 52,000 Indians, 43,000 South African whites, 3,000 Rhodesians and 27,000 black Africans. Northern Rhodesia recruited 41,000 blacks as military porters, and France had about half a million Africans among her colonial combatant troops, almost all of whom fought outside Africa.

The European way of war was enlightening, if horrifying, to the Africans. "You shoot from far, far away," commented a Matabele tribesman, "and do not know whom you are killing; that is unmanly. We prefer to fight man to man." To the Africans, it was astonishing how the missionaries were now asking them to forget what they had taught them for a century: that fighting and killing were wicked savage instincts which must be curbed. It was as though these missionaries had never preached love and gentleness, and never had a God named "the Prince of Peace."

Moreover, the white men fought in much the same way as the blacks—some brutally, some bravely, some with cowardice. At the beginning of the war, efforts were made to prevent blacks from having to kill white enemies: a British patrol, meeting a German one, would send a message down the line to the effect that the white man should shoot at the enemy white man, while the blacks were to shoot at each other. Since this was more efficacious in theory than in practice, the black man was told simply to shoot and kill the enemy, white or black.

Worse, the Christian victors were plainly unforgiving of the Christian vanquished. Even the missionaries of the defeated nation were not allowed to return.

Black nationalism, which had been stirring in Nigeria, in the French North African territories, in Senegal and in British West Africa before 1914, was given an immense boost by the discoveries of the war. It was to spread until most of the continent, over a period of four decades, was once more a land for the Africans.

◆

King Ferdinand of Rumania taking leave of his Prime Minister, Ionel Bratianu, before leaving for the front, 1916. By Underwood and Underwood.

The German prisoners' club room, Brest, France.

A company of French military cyclists. By Keystone View Company.

After the four-month-long battle of the Somme in 1916, the Allies had advanced seven miles in some places; in other places, none. For that, the British suffered 420,000 casualties; the French, more than 200,000; the Germans, 450,000.

French refugees fleeing from the Somme to Amiens.

French troops resting before an attack, Verdun, France, 1916.
By Underwood and Underwood.

German soldiers among the ruins

202

of Messines, near Ypres, Belgium.

A Moroccan cavalryman with the French troops at the front.

Woodrow Wilson was re-elected President in 1916 largely because he had "kept us out of war." Yet neutrality became increasingly untenable. German submarine warfare—which in 1915 had resulted in the sinking of the British vessel *Lusitania* with the loss of more than 1,100 lives, 128 of them American—sent eight American vessels to the bottom in early 1917. Rumania, which had surrendered as 1916 drew to a close, gave Germany vital supplies of oil and wheat. In March 1917, the Tsar was deposed and Russia's long-impending military collapse could not be concealed. With a clear numerical superiority in the West, Germany was ready to deal the knockout blow to the decimated and exhausted armies of Britain and France. Finally, on Good Friday, April 6, 1917, the United States went to war, sending almost 2 million soldiers to France by October 1918. The active resistance of fresh American troops quickly turned the tide against the Germans. At 11 A.M. on November 11, 1918, the cease-fire sounded along the Western Front, bringing World War I, which had killed 10 million persons, to an end.

American soldiers training with gas masks, Fort Dix, New Jersey. By Underwood and Underwood.

Above: Farewell at the train station.

*Right: American soldiers going home in a transport vessel.
By Underwood and Underwood.*

*Below: An American soldier with a French woman and
child, Brest, France.*

French cavalry officers looking up at a scout fighter plane.

King Albert of Belgium with Mrs. Woodrow Wilson touring a Belgian battlefield, June 1919.

After the War

A *wealthy Japanese family outside their home, Japan. By James Ricalton of Underwood and Underwood.*

The Great War gave Rumania territories it had long coveted—Bessarabia, Transylvania, Bukovina and southern Dobruja. Yet less than three decades later, when the world again went to war, Rumania was to be stripped of most of these lands. In Japan, the militarists, who had pushed for a surprise attack on Port Arthur in 1904 and who sought to colonize China during the Great War, would, twenty-three years after Armistice, order a surprise attack on the American naval base at Pearl Harbor, Hawaii. And in postwar India—a land where famine and starvation were perennially and brutally commonplace—the most devastating tactic Mohandas Karamchand Gandhi devised against the greatest empire in the world was the simple act of depriving himself of food.

Queen Marie of Rumania (left) with her eldest daughter, Elizabeth, outside the Hotel Ritz, Paris.

Mahatma Gandhi. By George Lewis of Keystone View Company.

A Chinese family. By Keystone View Company.

Women of Zanzibar. By Underwood and Underwood.

Three women, Atlantic City, New Jersey.

High school domestic-science room, Rockford, Illinois.
By Underwood and Underwood.

High school workshop, Rockford, Illinois.
By Underwood and Underwood.

Above: Coinage presses, the U.S. Mint. By Underwood and Underwood.

Left: Peach-canning factory, Visalia, California. By Phil Brigandi of Keystone View Company.

Below: Workers at a tire-manufacturing plant, Akron, Ohio. By Phil Brigandi of Keystone View Company.

Right: Women's lounge at a paper factory, Bangor, Maine. By Underwood and Underwood.

It was conceived during the American Civil War by Count
Ferdinand von Zeppelin (a balloon observer with the Union Army),
was launched by the Count in 1900, carried 40,000 passengers
over three continents during its heyday before the Great War,
gained notoriety during the war when it rained bombs on Allied
areas, and seemed relegated to history after the *Hindenburg* disaster
of 1937. More than four decades later, the dirigible—oddly
anachronistic and futuristic at the same time—is once more
dreamed of as the cargo airship of the future.

The Graf Zeppelin *flying over the pyramids of Gizeh.*
By George Lewis of Keystone View Company.